ASIAN LIBRARIES AND LIBRARIANSHIP

An Annotated Bibliography of Selected Books and Periodicals, and a Draft Syllabus

by
G. RAYMOND NUNN

The Scarecrow Press, Inc.
Metuchen, N.J.   1973

Library of Congress Cataloging in Publication Data

Nunn, Godfrey Raymond, 1918-
    Asian libraries and librarianship.

    1. Libraries--Asia--Bibliography. I. Title.
Z845.A1N85   016.021'0095   73-6629
ISBN 0-8108-0633-9

Copyright 1973 by G. Raymond Nunn

CONTENTS

	Preface	v
I.	GENERAL AND ASIA	1
II.	SOUTH ASIA	11
	Bangla Desh	12
	Ceylon (Sri Lanka)	14
	India	15
	Pakistan	31
III.	SOUTHEAST ASIA	39
	Burma	40
	Indonesia	42
	Laos	49
	Malaysia and Singapore	49
	Philippines	54
	Thailand	59
	Vietnam	62
IV.	EAST ASIA	65
	China	66
	Japan	75
	Korea	85

Appendix: Syllabus for a Course on Asian Libraries and Librarianship   91

Author and Title Index   117

Titles in Chinese, Japanese, Korean and Thai   133

PREFACE

During recent years considerable attention has been paid to the development of comparative librarianship as a field of study. At the University of Hawaii Graduate School of Library Studies, seminars in this field, with an emphasis on Asia, have been given since 1966, under the headings of Administration of Libraries in Asia, and Library Planning in Asia. The present work has been directly developed from the bibliography used in these seminars.

In the Spring of 1972, advantage was taken of my seminar in Administration of Libraries in Asia, to review the earlier bibliographies and to write annotations for the works selected for inclusion. Participants in the seminar were requested to write not only reports on a number of selected books and periodicals but also short annotations for inclusion in a possible bibliography. The annotations were checked against the reports, and in some cases against the books, and were edited. Together, they comprise approximately one-half of the entries in the present bibliography. I am very much indebted to the seminar participants who took part in this enterprise and who brought in many cases their local expertise to the task. Among them were Miss Mastini H. Prakoso, director of the Central Museum Library in Djakarta; Mr. Ramachandran of the National Library of Singapore; Mrs. Rugayah Rashid, librarian of the Institut Teknologi Mara, Kuala Lumpur; Mr. Peter Yeung of the University of Hong Kong Library; Mr. Muhammad Shoaib of the University of Kabul Library; Miss Tae-Sook Chung, Mr. Philip Walker, and Mr. Ronald Wagner. Mrs. Saingtong Ismail assisted with materials on Thai libraries. Professor T-H. Tsien, Mr. Shiro Saito, Dean Nasser Sharify and Dean Robert Stevens were able to assist with materials which would not have otherwise been available. The library staff of the University of Hawaii Asia Collection--in particular, its head, Miss Joyce Wright, and Mrs. Lynette Wageman, Mrs. Lan-hiang Char, Mr. Masato Matsui and Mr. Sam S. Hahn (who did the Chinese, Japanese and Korean calligraphy)--were of great assistance. I am also grateful for the help given me by Mr. Do Van Anh, the librarian of the Vien Khao Co in Saigon.

The bibliography, as it stands, lacks entries for the other three parts of the comparative librarianship equation, since it omits key works defining practice outside Asia in comparable developing countries, and materials on the United States and Canada, and on Europe, and finally for the social context, of which librarianship is only a very minor part. We should note, however, that in spite of the generally high standards in Western Europe, and in the United States and Canada, in many parts of these regions library service falls far below that of better examples in Asia, and we in the West can learn from the Asian experience, as also can Asian librarians learn from each other.

The major characteristic of this bibliography is that it cites books and periodicals only, although reports, and in some cases important papers read at conferences and major articles later given a distinct publication have been included. Periodical articles have been excluded. There are a number of reasons for this. In the first place, to have compiled an annotated bibliography including periodical articles would have been an enormous task, with some 20,000 entries for the period under review, from 1945. Secondly it was believed that these articles could best be located through bibliographies on libraries and librarianship which now exist for India, Pakistan, Thailand, the Philippines, China, Japan and Korea, and to important indexes such as Library Literature, Library and Information Science Abstracts, and the appropriate libraries and bibliography sections of the Bibliography of Asian Studies.

The second characteristic of the bibliography is that it is annotated. Every book listed has been examined personally by the compiler and almost every book in the bibliography now exists in one of the libraries of the University of Hawaii or is held by the compiler. Examination of bibliographies in the field of international librarianship has revealed too many faults due to lack of personal examination, and from misleading titles. The second reason for annotation is to bring out the fuller significance of the book. A title indicating "book development" may hide the fact that there is a substantial portion of the work devoted to libraries.

A third characteristic of this bibliography is that it refers in a balanced fashion to the important sources of information on librarianship existing in Asian languages. These are too frequently ignored, but students of librarianship must secure the needed linguistic assistance to interpret Asian language materials also if they wish to fully understand many specific country situations. Yet a fourth characteristic of the bibliography is that it draws attention to neglected sources of information on libraries and librarianship in the general reference literature on Asia. Statistical sources can give valuable information on the number of literates, schools, and urban centers of given sizes. Union lists of serials and library catalogs are another important source on library strengths and systems.

The study of each country was made along similar lines, taking up first an examination of publishing, and the generation and distribution of publications, followed by materials on libraries in general, then on special types of libraries, such as national libraries, university libraries, special libraries, public libraries and school libraries. The topics of cataloging and classification, library education, library associations and library building are also taken up. Periodicals are usually placed ahead of books and in each section materials are cited by date of publication. The bibliography has a country orientation and differs in structure from the syllabus, in the appendix, which is topic oriented, followed by a country consideration of each topic.

The responsibility for all entries rests with the compiler, and he will be most grateful for the readers' assistance in pointing out any error and omission.

G. Raymond Nunn
University of Hawaii
November 1972

I. GENERAL AND ASIA

PERIODICALS--Abstracts, Indexes and Lists

1. Library literature, 1933- . H. W. Wilson, 1936- monthly with cumulations.
    Only two Asian library journals are indexed currently, but there is a substantial number of references to Asian librarianship appearing in the non-Asia library literature. Earlier issues of the index are disappointing for their Asia coverage.

2. Library and information science abstracts, 1950- . London, Association of Special Libraries and Information Bureaus, 1950-   monthly.
    Abstracts from a wide range of international and American journals, including some 20 originating in Asia. Materials are arranged in a classified subject order, but with an adequate author and subject index.

3. Bibliography of Asian studies, 1956- . Ann Arbor, Association for Asian Studies, 1957-   annual.
    Useful since it indexes a wide range of Western language periodicals including those published in Asia, which are often not noticed elsewhere, and has had for many years sections dealing specifically with libraries and bibliography under the major Asian countries. Until 1969 an integral part of the Journal of Asian studies, but published independently since 1970. A cumulated edition Cumulative bibliography of Asian studies, 1941-1965, author bibliography (Boston, G. K. Hall, 1969, 4 v.) and Cumulative bibliography of Asian studies, 1941-1965, subject bibliography (Boston, G. K. Hall, 1970, 4 v.) have been published. A further cumulation will cover the years 1966-1970.

4. International Federation for Documentation. Library and documentation journals, third revised edition,

The Hague, 1968. 88 p. (FID publication 433.)
Lists 517 periodicals by country, with 58 countries represented. For each entry the English translation of the title, issuing body, frequency, subscription rate, language and information on contents given. Russian titles are not translated. Subject index, but no title index. More comprehensive than Winckler's Library periodicals directory, especially in its emphasis on documentation.

PERIODICALS--Individual Titles

5. UNESCO bulletin for libraries, 1947- . Paris, UNESCO, bi-monthly.
Articles stress daily operations of various types of libraries, problem solving, bibliography, reference, documentation and archives. Practicing librarians in various countries offer basic advice in setting up and operating libraries.

6. Libri; international library review and communications, 1950- . Copenhagen, Munksgaard, quarterly.
The journal of the International Federation of Library Associations, which is soliciting and aiding further Asian participation. A number of articles have appeared on Asian library problems.

7. Library trends, 1952- . Urbana, University of Illinois Library School, monthly.
Each issue is devoted to a single theme usually of universal interest. Frequent publication of articles on developments in Asia related to the central topic of an issue.

8. Franklin Book Programs, Inc. Report. New York, 1953- annual.
Progress and future plans in the development of book publication in developing countries, including reports from project centers at Dacca, Djakarta, Kabul and Lahore.

9. UNESCO. Regional Centre for Reading Materials in South Asia, Karachi. Newsletter. Karachi, 1959-
Concerned with libraries and publishing mostly in Southern Asia, but draws on experience in other areas relevant to Southern Asia problems.

General and Asia 3

10. UNESCO. Bibliography, documentation, terminology. 1961- . Paris, bi-monthly.
Reports meetings of international scope dealing with books, and carries information updating bibliographic services throughout the world, international and national book activities, and archives.

11. Publishers' international yearbook, world directory of book publishers. London, A. P. Wales, 1961- annual.
Fifth edition for 1968 noted, with far fewer publishers for many countries than those noted in Publishers' international directory, but these are recognizable as publishers in distinction to booksellers for many Asian countries.

12. UNESCO. Statistical yearbook. Paris, 1963- .
Of special interest are tables listing the numbers of libraries and their holdings by category, a table listing current expenditures on libraries in each category. Listings are by country. Tables of book production statistics date from 1955, showing number of titles published in the classes of the Universal Decimal Classification, and by language, titles, and copies, by first editions, text books, children's books, translations by country, and by original language, and translations from languages most frequently translated.

13. United Nations. Economic Commission for Asia and the Far East. Statistical yearbook for Asia and the Far East, 1968- . Bangkok, 1969- .
Contains valuable information related to library and book development in Asia, with statistics going back to 1958.

14. Libraries in international development. Washington, International Relations Office, American Library Association, 1967-1972. 10 issues a year.
A newsletter on library and related programs for the developing countries, but with substantial reference to Asia. Items are brief, but help to update other sources.

15. International library review, 1969- . New York, Academic Press, quarterly.
Deals with research and progress in international and comparative librarianship, usually with at least

16. The Far East and Australasia: a survey and directory of Asia and the Pacific. London, Europa Publications, 1969- .
   The only directory giving current information for Asian countries, with some 20 percent devoted to Australasia and the Pacific. For each country there is a short introduction, and information on a number of matters. Of particular interest are its survey of education, and lists of learned institutions, research institutes, museums and universities, with addresses. May be regarded as a substitute for The world of learning for the Asia area.

PUBLISHING

17. Trans-Pacific Conference on Scholarly Publishing, 1st. Honolulu, 1962. Trans-Pacific scholarly publishing; a symposium. Honolulu, University of Hawaii Press, East-West Center Press, 1963. 273p.
   A three-part collection of papers presented at the conference on scholarly publishing. The first part consists of background papers on historical and current trends and problems, the second part is a set of papers describing the North American experience, and the third part arises out of international experience with cooperation and aid.

18. Lee, Margaret. The book programs sponsored by the Asia Foundation, UNESCO and the United States Information Agency in the Far East. River Forest, Illinois, 1964. 39p.
   A paper submitted at Rosary College, Department of Library Science in partial fulfillment of requirements for degree of Master of Arts in Library Science, and discusses the Asia Foundation Books for Asian students program, UNESCO book coupons, Clearing House, technical assistance and USIA libraries, translation projects and book distribution programs.

19. Meeting of Experts on Book Production and Distribution in Asia, Tokyo. 1966. Final report. Paris, UNESCO, 1966. 44p.

General and Asia   5

   An assessment of Asia's book needs. Deals with
   the development of publishing for education and special problems of children's literature, scholarly publishing, scientific publishing and paperbacks. Also described are the problems of structure of the publishing industry in Asia, as well as distribution problems, trade barriers, translation and copyright problems which influence the international flow of information.

20. UNESCO. Book development in Asia; a report on the production and distribution of books in the region. Paris, UNESCO, 1967. 70p.
   The first section is a report of the Tokyo 1966 meeting, followed by a section of statistical tables and summary statement. The appendix contains a costing analysis.

21. Publishers' international directory; internationales Verlagsadressbuch. 5th ed., 1972. Part 2, America, Asia and Oceania. New York, R. R. Bowker, 1972. p. 835-957.
   Lists publishers in Asia, including West Asia, although it is very questionable if all entries in sections for Indonesia and India are active publishers, as distinct from booksellers.

22. World directory of booksellers, and international guide to booksellers. 1st ed., London, A. P. Wales, 1970. 911 p.
   Arranged by country, place, then by name of publisher. Language and subject materials sold noted.

LIBRARIES

23. Asheim, Lester. Librarianship in the developing countries. Urbana, University of Illinois Press, 1966. 95 p.
   Discusses the cultural differences which have bearing on how American librarians can contribute to libraries in developing countries. Emphasizes the major contrasts with American libraries. America does have important concepts to offer, and the author suggests a partnership for a two-way exchange.

24. Meeting of Experts on the National Planning of Library Services in Asia, Colombo, 1967. Main working document. Paris, 1967. 88 p. --. Final report. Paris, 1968. 31 p.

The main document sets the background for planning a national library service in Ceylon, and details planning requirements for the role of library service in educational, economic and social development. The necessary elements for long-term planning are listed. The final report summarizes and makes recommendations for Ceylon, then for UNESCO and its member states.

25. Ranganathan, Shiyala Ramamrita. Free book service for all; an international survey. Bangalore, Mysore Library Association, 1968. 464 p.

An outline of the philosophy behind public library service, and a survey of application internationally. 37 countries are surveyed, of which 17 are from Asia. Most detailed information for India.

26. International library directory. 3d ed. London, A. P. Wales, 1968. 1221 p.

A world listing of libraries by country and by city within the country. Gives data about the library including the name, address, type of library, number of volumes, librarian, scope of collection, languages collected, exchange activities, type of periodicals collection. 22 Asian countries are represented. Earlier editions are useful for historical purposes.

27. Kent, Allen and Harold Lancour. Encyclopedia of library and information sciences. New York, Dekker, 1968- mult. vols.

Relatively minor in scope for its up-to-date coverage of the Asian library scene.

28. Kaser, David. Library development in eight Asian countries. Metuchen, New Jersey, Scarecrow Press, 1969. 243 p.

Describes the current (1966-67) state of library activities in Korea, the Philippines, Republic of China (Taiwan), Republic of Viet-Nam, Laos, Thailand, Indonesia, Federation of Malaysia and Republic of Singapore. Description includes background material and information about school, academic,

General and Asia   7

   public, special, foreign and national libraries, information on bibliographic control and services, professional associations, library education and other library functions for each of these countries. Based largely on A. I. D. surveys.

29. Avicenne, Paul. Bibliographic services throughout the world, 1960-1964. Paris, UNESCO, 1969. 228 p. (UNESCO bibliographic handbook series.)
   Based on replies to a questionnaire or on information in UNESCO Bibliography, documentation, terminology, and includes nearly all Asian countries, with statements on the status of their national bibliography. Updates a report by Robert L. Collison Bibliographical services throughout the world, 1950-59.

30. Simsova, S. and M. Mackee. A handbook of comparative librarianship. Hamden, Connecticut, Shoestring Press, 1970. 413 p.
   Discussion of the methods of comparative study of libraries and a beginning guide to sources, including places or organizations to consult within a country such as national libraries or official bodies, as well as reference sources such as directories, yearbooks, etc., and background bibliography.

31. World guide to libraries; internationales Bibliothekshandbuch. 3d ed. Part 4, Africa, Asia, Oceania. New York, R. R. Bowker, 1970. p. 1711-2281.
   Criteria for inclusion is a collection of 30,000 volumes for a general library, or 3000 volumes for a special library. Information given includes name and address, number of volumes, type of library. 125 pages on Asian libraries, including those in West Asia.

32. Chandler, George. Libraries in the East; an international and comparative study. New York, Seminar Press, 1971. 214 p.
   Surveys the recommendations made by UNESCO for library service development, and compares these to the situation in the Middle East, Pakistan, India, Thailand, Hong Kong, and Japan, with an emphasis on libraries in urban situations. Particular emphasis is given to Japanese libraries. Contains a valuable bibliography and a general compara-

tive survey essay on libraries in Asia.

NATIONAL LIBRARIES

33. UNESCO. Guide to national bibliographical information centres. Paris, 1970. 195 p.
    Lists the main national bibliographical centers of general scope or specializing in such fields as education, human and social sciences, etc. Provides directory-type information on the centers, noting publications and reproduction services.

UNIVERSITY LIBRARIES

34. Gelfand, Morris A. University libraries for developing countries. Paris, UNESCO, 1968. 157 p.
    Intended as a technical guide for those establishing small university libraries, and suitable as an informative background for government and university administrators and faculty responsible for the development of the library. Covers administrative, technical, service areas, and role of library in society.

SPECIAL LIBRARIES

35. UNESCO Seminar on Scientific Documentation in South and Southeast Asia, Delhi, 1961. Scientific documentation in South and Southeast Asia; a survey of a regional seminar held in New Delhi from 7th to 16th March, 1961, under the auspices of UNESCO and the Government of India. New Delhi, UNESCO South Asia Science Cooperation Office, 1963. 47 p.
    Summaries of the organization of the seminar and abstracts of reports on the position of scientific documentation in Asian countries, including Japan, together with technical background papers by UNESCO experts and listing of final proposals.

36. U.S. Library of Congress. Science and Technology Division. A guide to the world's abstracting and indexing services in science and technology. Washington, 1963. 183 p.
    Lists continuing bibliographical services aiding in

General and Asia

the documentation of the scientific and technical literature of the world. Arranged alphabetically, and also by a subject-classified scheme with country and subject indexes. Major contribution from Japan.

37. UNESCO. World guide to science information and documentation services. Paris, 1965. 211 p.
Intended as a guide to services in the natural sciences, since technology is found in a separate volume. Not comprehensive, but refers to more complete national sources. Directory-type information for centers. Indexed by subject.

PUBLIC LIBRARIES

38. Seminar on the Development of Public Libraries in Asia. Delhi, 1955. Public libraries for Asia; the Delhi seminar. Paris, UNESCO, 1956. 165 p. (UNESCO Public Library manuals 7)
A study of public library development in Asia, concerned with organization, at the national, public and rural levels, publishing and reading lists, and service for children. An appendix surveys the public library situation country by country.

LIBRARY EDUCATION

39. Bonn, George S. Library education and training in developing countries. Honolulu, East-West Center Press, 1966. 199 p.
Working papers of a conference on library education and training in East and South Asia. The U.S. participants provided papers on recent U.S. efforts to develop foreign librarians, and Asian library educators presented the current state of library education in their countries.

LIBRARY COOPERATION AND AID

40. Seminar on the International Exchange of Publications in the Indo-Pacific Area, Tokyo. Exchange of ideas; East and West meet the challenge; Final report of the seminar on the international exchange of publications in the Indo-Pacific area, November

4-11, 1957, Tokyo. Tokyo, The National Diet Library, 1958. 297 p.

Proceedings of the conference, reporting experience in national exchange services. Preliminary draft conventions developed. Selected working documents describe programs of participant countries.

II. SOUTH ASIA

BANGLA DESH

PERIODICALS

41. Catalogue of books and periodicals registered in the Province of E. Pakistan during the quarter ending .... Dacca gazette, appendix.
    The fullest statement for the publications of the former East Pakistan, including coverage of books, periodicals and official publications, mostly in English or Bengali. Last issues noted cover 1967 imprints.

42. The Eastern librarian. Dacca, East Pakistan Library Association, 1966-   quarterly.
    Emphasis is almost completely on library developments in Pakistan, with some articles on activities in East Pakistan and elsewhere. Short notes on the East Pakistan Library Association.

BOOKS

43. Hulbert, James A. Development of libraries. Dacca, U.S. Information Service, 1963. 34 p.
    A comparative study of library development and services in different countries, emphasizing libraries in the United States and the former East Pakistan. Emphasis is on library development and application of principles and professional criteria.

44. Bengali Academy, Dacca. What women read in East Pakistan; a survey. Karachi, National Book Centre of Pakistan, 1964. 60 p.
    Based on a questionnaire to educated and literate women in East Pakistan, and analyzing type of reading material read and subject interests.

45. Bengali Academy, Dacca. What people read in East Pakistan; a survey. Karachi, National Book Centre of Pakistan, 1965. 91 p.

Bangla Desh

Intended at first to cover men only, but later extended in a fresh survey of East Pakistan analyzing reading habits, and reasons for reading. Inferiority of East Pakistan publishing compared with Indian publishing is pointed out.

46. Khan, Muhammed Siddiq. The need for public library development; being the proceedings of the Seminar. Dacca, East Pakistan Library Association, 1966. 151 p.

A series of papers on the need for a public library service, public libraries and education, public library legislation, present status of public libraries in Pakistan, and a plan for development. IFLA Public Library working paper (1953), British Public Libraries and Museum Bill (1964) and UNESCO Public Library Manifesto appended.

47. Syed, M. A. Public libraries in East Pakistan. Dacca, Green Book House, 1968. 116 p.

A historical survey, with emphasis on the period since 1947 is followed by a discussion on the ways public libraries could be developed. Appendix A lists public libraries in East Pakistan, and Appendix B is a model Public Libraries Act. Full bibliography.

48. Huq, A. M. Abdul. A study of Bengali Muslim names to ascertain the feasibility of application of a mechanistic rule for their arrangement. Pittsburgh, University of Pittsburgh, 1970. 87 p.

A Ph. D. thesis in librarianship analyzes Bengali Muslim names, and their frequency. The thesis suggests rules for arrangement in alphabetical files.

CEYLON (SRI LANKA)

49. Ceylon. Department of Census and Statistics. <u>Statistical abstract of Ceylon,</u> 1949- . Colombo, Government Publications Bureau, 1949- .
    Useful for information on the numbers of books published, by language and by subject, also for expenditure on public libraries, and enrollments in schools and universities.

50. Ceylon. Office of the Registrar of Books and Newspapers. <u>Catalogue of books</u> ... 1960-64? Colombo, Government Press, 1960-64?
    An excellent bibliographical record continuing the <u>Ceylon Government Gazette</u>, Part V (1885-) and including some 4000 entries a year.

51. <u>Ceylon national bibliography,</u> v. 1- . 1963- . Nugegoda, National Bibliography Branch, Department of the Government Archivist, 1964- .
    May be regarded as a continuation of the <u>Catalogue of books</u>. A more current, but selected list, is provided by the U.S. Library of Congress. American Libraries Book Procurement Center, New Delhi. <u>Accessions list, Ceylon,</u> 1967- .

14

INDIA

52. India (Republic). Central Statistical Organization. Statistical abstract of the Indian Union, 1949- . Delhi, Manager of Publications, Government of India, 1950-   annual.
  Compiled from official sources, and information for the year published and national aggregates for 5 or 10 year periods. Information is included on books published by languages and printing presses.

PUBLISHING--Periodicals

53. The Indian publisher and bookseller. Bombay, 1950- monthly.
  A trade journal containing articles and editorials relating to the book trade, and with many regular features of a current nature. Publications of the Month contains much information on current Indian publications in English, but is not cumulated.

54. India (Republic). Office of the Registrar of Newspapers. Press in India. Part II, 1956- . New Delhi, Ministry of Information and Broadcasting, 1957-   Annual.
  A catalog of serials arranged by State, frequency of publication and language. Detailed information included in each entry about date of establishment, publisher, price, printer.

55. Indian national bibliography, 1958- . Calcutta, National Library, 1958- .
  Commenced publication as a quarterly, since January 1964 has been published monthly, and includes works in English and other major Indian languages, recorded in a romanized alphabetization. National and State publications are included. Arrangement is by the Dewey Decimal Classification, but Colon numbers are also given.

15

56. Booktraders, Calcutta, 1959-   quarterly.
Contains articles on bookselling and related fields, and features such as book reviews, book news around the world, rare-book want list. Each issue has a special theme.

57. Publishers' monthly, New Delhi, 1959- .
Contains articles and editorials about current problems in publishing and allied fields in India. Each issue also contains book reviews of books published in India. The regular "Books of the Month" section is very brief and highly selective for recent or forthcoming publications. Text is mostly in English, but some of the articles and advertisements are in Hindi.

58. Indian books; a yearly bibliography of Indian books published or reprinted in the English language. Delhi, Researchco, 1969-   annual.
Attempts to cover the problem that the Indian national bibliography is neither cumulated nor published annually, but it excludes books not in English, children's books, school textbooks and official publications. Publisher's directory is appended. 1971 issue noted.

PUBLISHING--Books

59. Hollister, John N. The Lucknow Publishing House, 1861-1961; a brief history. Lucknow, Lucknow Publishing House, 1961. 212 p.
Less than one fifth of this book deals with the situation after 1945 of this publishing house closely associated with the Methodist Church in India.

60. Parkash, Dewan Ram. Directory of booksellers and publishers, 1963. Calcutta, R. P. Bookwala and Co., 1963. 163 p.
Edition of a directory first published in 1950, with booksellers and publishers arranged by town. The second part is a list of newspapers and periodicals, arranged first by language, then by frequency of publication.

61. Thatachari, C. S. S. Book trade manual for South Asian countries. Madras, Book Industry Council

India   17

of South India, 1963. 140 p.
Based on the reports of the Booksellers' Training Courses conducted under the UNESCO Project on Reading Materials in India, Pakistan, Burma, Ceylon and Iran. A practical discussion of the techniques of bookstore management.

62. Sankaranarayanan, N. Book distribution and promotion problems in South Asia. Madras, Higginbothams, 1965? 278 p.
A collection of papers discussing book distribution in South Asia, Burma and Iran, distribution in the advanced countries, book marketing procedures, training courses in bookselling and the role of libraries.

63. Singh, Mohinder. Government publications of India, a survey of their nature, bibliographical control and distribution system. Delhi, Metropolitan Book Co., 1967. 270 p.
A partial guide to the publications of the Indian national government, the largest single publisher in India. A general introduction to government report writing is followed by a department by department description of important publications and methods of procurement. Information on State publications not given.

64. Seminar on Book Publishing, Delhi, 1969. Report. New Delhi, Federation of Publishers and Booksellers Association in India, 1969. 182 p.
Papers presented at the seminar dealing with the problems of publishing and bookselling in India. Eleven resolutions state the problems and their solution as seen by the industry.

LIBRARIES--Bibliography

65. Kaula, Prithvi Nath. Indian library literature; a bibliography of publications. Delhi, Delhi Library Association, 1956. 22 p. (Delhi Library Association. English series 1.)
Some 170 books and periodicals are listed in a detailed subject arrangement.

66. Prasher, Ram Gopal. Indian library literature; an

annotated bibliography. New Delhi, Today and Tomorrows, 1971. 504 p.
   Contains over 3,500 entries, including books, periodical articles and dissertations, published from 1955. Some entries are annotated. Arranged in Dewey Decimal Classification order, with subject and author indexes.

LIBRARIES--Periodicals

67. Indian librarian. Jallundur, 1946- quarterly.
   Publishes articles relating to library problems in India, and review Indian and Western books. Indexed in Library literature, and Library and information science abstracts.

68. Annals of library science, New Delhi, Indian National Scientific Documentation Center, 1954- .
   Changed its name in 1964 to Annals of library science and documentation, and is concerned with problems of scientific documentation on a worldwide basis. Only of secondary interest to librarians. Indexed in Library and information science abstracts.

69. Indian Library Association. The Journal. Calcutta, Ramakrishna Mission of Culture, 1955-1964, quarterly.
   Superseded Abgila, 1949-1953, and was in turn superseded by Indian Library Association, The Bulletin, 1965- . Contains articles of a nontechnical nature on problems of librarians and administrators in India. Minor part of each issue concerned with internal business of the Indian Library Association.

70. Library herald. Delhi, Delhi Library Association, 1958- quarterly.
   Primarily concerned with problems of Indian libraries, by librarians well known in India and internationally. Issues are often concentrated on a particular problem. Indexed in Library literature and Library and information science abstracts.

71. Indian Association of Special Libraries and Information Centres. IASLIC special publications. Calcutta,

India   19

   1960?- .
   This series covers a wide range of topics on
   Indian libraries and librarianship: no. 2 (1961)
   discusses the rendering of Indic names, and contains a bibliography on the subject, no. 5 (1965) is
   concerned with education for librarianship in India,
   no. 6 (1966) with document and data processing and
   problems of library associations, and no. 7 (1966)
   with classification, inter-library loan and social
   science documentation in India.

72. Herald of library science, Banares, Ranganathan Endowment for Library Science, 1962-   quarterly.
   Includes many articles by Ranganathan as well
   as other prominent Indian and foreign librarians.
   Many of the articles by Ranganathan are on cataloging. Indexed in Library literature and Library and
   information science abstracts.

73. Indian Library Association. The Bulletin. New Delhi,
   1965-   quarterly.
   Supersedes Indian Library Association's. The
   Journal. Contains many excellent articles on problems of libraries in India and Asia. Part of each
   issue concerned with internal business of the Indian
   Library Association. Indexed in Library literature
   and Library and information science abstracts.

LIBRARIES--Books

74. Indian Library Association. Directory of Indian libraries, 1944. 2d. ed. (rev. & enl.). Calcutta,
   Indian Library Association, 1944. 75 p. (Indian
   Library Association. Publication no. 2.)
   1500 questionnaires were sent to libraries, and
   only 320 replied. Information for an additional 199
   was found from other sources. Arranged by province, with date of foundation of library, budget,
   collection information, and name of director.

75. Indian Library Association. Indian library directory,
   3d ed. Delhi, Indian Library Association, 1951.
   117 p. (Indian Library Association. English series
   4.)
   More of an analytic survey than a directory,
   363 libraries are listed, all with a collection size

of over 5000 volumes. Information is given on budget, collections and staff. Further parts show the geographic distribution of libraries, kinds of libraries, survey library associations, and programs of library training. A short bibliography on librarianship in India is followed by a short who's who in Indian librarianship, with entries for some 90 librarians.

76. Kaula, Prithvi Nath. Library movement in India. Delhi, Delhi Library Association, 1958. 153 p.
Contains the papers presented for discussion at the first Delhi Library Conference in 1957 on the library movement in India. The first part is concerned with library development in India, and the second on the library movement in five of the States.

77. Ranaganathan, Shiyala Ramamrita. Library administration. New York, Asia Publishing House, 1959. 674 p. (Ranganathan Series in Library science 3.)
Second edition of 1935 work, more concerned with routine procedure in libraries than with administration. Valuable in that it gives insights into Indian library management.

78. Chakravarty, N. C. Library movement in India. Delhi, Hindustan Publishing Corp., 1962. 37 p.
A brief and comprehensive account of the history of library development in India since 1850, traces library history from the formation of the first library in Baroda in 1910 to the different types of public, special and national libraries that have developed. Very little interpretation. In some cases the author merely enumerates the number of library association meetings and activities that took place.

79. Ranganathan, Shiyala Ramamrita. The organization of libraries. Calcutta, New York, Oxford University Press, 1963. 189 p.
In three parts, on library and education, library practice, and national library system. Each part is further subdivided. The relation between library organization and education, and the techniques of library science are discussed. There is a chapter on Ranganathan's Colon Classification.

80. Bengal Library Association. Library service in India today: a symposium on the library developments in

eastern India. Calcutta, 1963. 127 p.
Organized by the Bengal Library Association and USIS Calcutta in 1960 to review library development in Bengal and to look into similar developments in other States. The following are discussed: Library service in schools and children's libraries, public libraries in relation to the community, bookmobile service.

81. Bengal Library Association. Directory sub-committee. West Bengal library directory. Calcutta, 1963. 482 p.
A list of 3968 libraries with addresses arranged by type of library and then by town, and with details presented in tabular form, i.e. staffing, number of books, income, etc. Represents some 50 per cent of the questionnaires sent out.

82. New India directory of libraries and educational institutions. New Delhi, New Book Society of India, n.d. 160 p.
Coverage for India, Pakistan, Burma and Ceylon, but information, except for a short list for Pakistan, very scanty for countries other than India. Arrangement of the major section, a list of libraries in India, in 136 pages, is alphabetical by name of institution, and there are nearly 7000 entries with addresses.

83. Chakravarty, N. C. Libraries in fourth five-year plan. Delhi, 1964. 14 p.
Outlines a program of library development under the plan, and observes that former plans have done little to provide for the nation-wide integrated system that had been drawn up in 1951. An outline to build a basic structure is presented.

84. Kalia, D. R. Libraries in fourth five-year plan. Delhi, 1964. 23 p.
The Indian library oyotem lacks central planning, coordination and direction, and the author outlines a plan to give this. Contains four different plans, each to be funded either by the Central Government, the State governments or jointly sponsored. Appendices contain statistics on libraries in India.

85. Delhi Library Association. Directory of libraries and

who's who in library profession in Delhi. Delhi, 1964. 91 p. (Delhi Library Association. English series 3.)
Lists 104 libraries, with information on subject emphasis, size of collection, users and hours of opening. 39 major libraries did not respond to the questionnaire. 218 librarians are listed with information on their positions and educational background.

86. Sen, N. B. Development of libraries in New India. New Delhi, New Book Society of India, 1965. 355 p.
Contains 57 articles on the principles of librarianship in general and on library systems and the book trade in India. Whole book lacks balance and scholarly treatment. On the other hand some articles present information not found elsewhere.

87. Indian Library Association. Proceedings of XIV All-India Library Conference held in Patna, from 10-15th April 1964. Delhi, 1965. 120 p.
Includes the papers submitted, summary of discussions and resolutions passed at the conference. Part I contains the addresses of principal librarians and government ministers and Part II contains papers submitted on State librarianship and State library legislation. Part III is a miscellaneous section.

88. Khandavala, Vidyut K and M. K. R. Nayudu. Directory of libraries, publishers and booksellers in the city of Bombay. Bombay, S. N. D. T. Women's University, 1965. 75 p.
Lists libraries, divided into academic, special, public, government and commercial firms, and publishers and booksellers in Bombay. Information on libraries includes address, size of collection, subject and language emphasis and name of librarian.

89. Indian Council for Library Development. A union list of learned American serials in Indian libraries. Delhi, 1966. 410 p.
Lists 2584 serials, with locations and holdings in 161 libraries, a useful clue to relative strengths of library collections.

90. Sen, N. B. Progress of libraries in Free India. New Delhi, New Book Society of India, 1967. 247 p.

India 23

Written to provide additional material to the author's Development of libraries in Free India, and contains 28 articles covering a wide range of topics on libraries and library development in India. Articles are more substantial than in the previous book, but the book still has many organizational defects.

91. Khosla, Raj K. Men of library science and libraries in India. New Delhi, Premier Publications, 1967. 1 v. (various paging).
Lists some 650 librarians with their biographies, 1400 libraries, with a short description, noting in some cases the size of collection, and a final section with a listing of some 3000 academic libraries, 360 special libraries, and 1100 State and public libraries.

92. Sadhu, S. W. Library legislation in India; a historical and comparative study. New Delhi, Sagar Publications, 1967. 285 p.
The first section traces the law of libraries, the second is a comparative study of the various aspects of the Madras Public Library Act of 1948, the Uttar Pradesh Public Libraries Act 1960, and the Model Public Libraries Bill of 1962. Section three consists of six public library acts of a number of states of India.

93. Indian Association of Special Libraries and Information Centres. Seventh IASLIC Conference, 27-30 December 1967, Souvenir. Delhi, University of Delhi, 1968? 85 p.
A series of reports on libraries in Delhi, IASLIC, the Delhi Library Association, Government of India Library Association, library training and the book trade in Delhi.

94. Mookerjee, Subodh Kumar. Development of libraries and library science in India. Calcutta, World Press Private, 1969. 534 p.
Survey of library development in India, covering the library movement, copyright, academic and special libraries, public libraries, bibliography, organization and administration, and public libraries and national development. Appendices contain an expansion of the Dewey Decimal Classification for

Indic subjects, and a discussion of library education in India.

NATIONAL LIBRARY

95. Calcutta. National Library. Report. Calcutta, 1903- .
In the issue of 1960/61 examined the progress of the Library was recorded for the period April 1, 1960 to March 31, 1961. 19 appendices of statistics survey the work of different divisions.

96. Kesavan, B. S. India's National Library. Calcutta, National Library, 1961. 300 p.
Traces the history, growth, administrative arrangements, library collections and equipment, national bibliography and problems of India's National Library. Also includes 15 appendices, annotated selected bibliography, and many plates and illustrations describing services and sections of the Library.

UNIVERSITY LIBRARIES

97. India (Republic). University Grants Commission. Handbook of universities in India, 1963. New Delhi, 1964. 275 p.
Provides general information on universities in India, with the first part giving general information about India and the University Grants Commission, and with three parts listing 70 universities, with information on their administration and enrollment.

98. White, Carl M. A survey of the University of Delhi Library. Delhi, Planning Unit, University of Delhi, 1965. 184 p.
Reports on the condition and needs of the Delhi University Library, with such topics as the University Library in perspective, conditions favorable to success, the book collections, the government of the library, general administration and library cooperation. Appended are statistical tables and figures.

99. India (Republic). University Grants Commission. University and college libraries. New Delhi, 1965. 228 p.

India 25

Contains the report of the Library Committee of the University Grants Commission, concerned with finance, acquisitions, stock preservation, personnel, buildings, and also includes the proceedings of the 1959 seminar "From publisher to reader" emphasizing the role of the library.

100. Seminar of University Librarians in India, Jaipur, 1966. Proceedings of first seminar of university librarians in India, held at the Rajasthan University, Jaipur, from 16th to 19th November, 1966. Jaipur, 1967, 4 v.
The second and third volumes contain papers read at the seminar, on the role of the university library, inter-library cooperation, the University Grants Commission, the librarian, coordination between college and university libraries, standards, and thoughts on accelerating the development of university libraries.

101. Trehan, G. L. Administration and organization of college libraries in India. Delhi, Sterling Publishers, 1969. 252 p.
In spite of the title, much of the book discusses the general principles of college library administration and the development and organization of college libraries in the United States and the United Kingdom, and compares these with practice in India. Appendices contain student use of libraries in the Punjab colleges, and a one-day survey of library use.

SPECIAL LIBRARIES

102. Indian Association of Special Libraries and Information Centres, Calcutta. IASLIC bulletin, 1956- . Calcutta, 1956- quarterly.
Articles on special library service, documentation, information retrieval and services. Abstracts of articles appear in Library and information science abstracts.

103. Indian Association of Special Libraries and Information Centers. Directory of special and research libraries in India. Calcutta, Oxford Book and Stationery Co., 1962. 282 p.

Lists 173 special libraries in India, with each entry providing statistics in 20 areas such as shelving space, reading room size, budget, classification scheme used, etc. Subject index, place index and name index included.

104. Ranganathan, Shiyali Ramamrita. Documentation and its facets. Bombay, Asia Publishing House, 1963. 639 p.

Consists of 70 articles on all aspects of documentation largely relating to Indian conditions. The first three parts are theoretical and historical, and the last discuss the future and problems of documentation. Very detailed, neglects to cover techniques of classification, cataloging, reference service, machine coding.

105. Saha, J. Special libraries and information services in India and the U.S.A. Metuchen, New Jersey, Scarecrow Press, 1969. 216 p.

The first part deals with India, and the second with the United States. The contents and aims of special libraries and documentation activities in both countries are discussed, and in addition there are useful chapters on education for librarianship and documentation bibliography and library associations in India and the USA.

106. Indian National Scientific Documentation Centre. The directory of scientific research institutions in India, 1969. New Delhi, 1969. 1120 p.

1374 questionnaires were sent out, and this book is based on 768 replies and on information from other sources. Covers nearly all the major research and development activities in India.

PUBLIC LIBRARIES

107. Delhi. Public Library. Report. 1951/52- .

The issue of the report examined covered the period April 1, 1967, to March 31, 1968. It is in five sections: general review, Delhi Library Board, administrative services, technical services and readers' services. Ten appendices of library statistics.

108. Gardner, Frank M. The Delhi Public Library, an

India 27

evaluation report. Paris, UNESCO, 1957. 94 p.
(UNESCO Public library manuals 8.)
Consists of 17 chapters, each of which describes and evaluates a particular aspect of the Library. Important aspects surveyed are administrative and organizational problems, occupational and educational background of the members, extent and kind of use. The purpose of the report is not only to assist in the further development of the Library, but also of public libraries in other parts of Asia.

109. Bala, Satyanarayana K. The law of public libraries in India. Allahabad, Law Book Co., 1962. 157 p.
Presents in full the Acts, Rules and provisions of other enactments relating to Indian library legislation. The author comments on these, together with a history of the Indian library movement and a summary of the recommendations of the Advisory Committee for Libraries set up in 1955.

110. Mittal, S. R. Organizing a village library. New Delhi, National Council of Education Research and Training, National Fundamental Education Centre, 1964. 28 p.
Outlines the functions and organization of a village library. Takes the special patrons the village library serves and the special problems it faces into consideration when it suggests the guidelines for its operation.

111. India (Republic). Planning Commission. Working Group on Libraries. A survey of public library services in India. Delhi, Indian Library Association, 1965. 66 p.
Based on data collected from government-financed public libraries in 15 Indian States, contains a ten-page written summary, and 50 tables.

112. Nagar, Lal Murari. Public library movement in Baroda, 1901-1949. Columbia, International Library Center, 1967. 371 p.
Examines the growth and decline of public libraries in Baroda, and is the first exhaustive study of the subject throwing light and insight to library development in developing nations.

113. Trehan, G. L. Modern public library movement and

library legislation for Punjab. Chandigarh, Library Literature House, 1967. 46 p. (Library literature in India, series no. 1.)
In two parts, the first dealing with the background of public libraries in the Punjab, and the second with their present status and need for a State Public Library Law.

SCHOOL LIBRARIES

114. Uttar Pradesh, India. Board of High School and Intermediate Education. List of books for libraries of high schools and intermediate colleges, corrected up to May 1959. Allahabad, Supt. Printing and Stationery, 1960. 136 p.
Some 4000 titles are arranged by subject or under 11 Indian languages.

115. All India Seminar on School Libraries, Bangalore, India, 1962. All India seminar on school libraries. New Delhi, Directorate of Extension Programs for Secondary Education, National Council of Education Research and Training, 1962. 45 p.
The seminar was conducted by Dr. S. R. Ranganathan, the objectives of education, creative as opposed to transmissive education, the correlation of class work and library work, and the roles of teacher, headmaster, and librarian were discussed. Valuable suggestions made for the improvement of library services in the Indian secondary school.

116. Trehan, G. L. Administration and organization of school libraries in India. Jullundur, Sterling Publishers, 1965. 291 p.
Emphasizes the use of the library rather than library techniques in the narrower sense, so that the school library can become a more effective instrument of education. Current trends in school librarianship outside India are also discussed, as well as the educational aims and functions of the school library, steps in planning the school library, and role of the school librarian and teacher.

India 29

CATALOGING AND CLASSIFICATION

117. Calcutta. National Library. Author table for Indian names. Calcutta, Government of India Press, 1961. 255 p.
   The use of the Cutter author table leads to unwieldy numbers for non-Anglo-Saxon names, and this table helps to solve this problem for Indian names.

118. Ranganathan, Shiyali Ramamrita. Elements of library classification, based on lectures delivered at the University of Bombay in December 1944, and in the schools of librarianship in Great Britain in December 1956. Bombay, Asia Publishing House, 1962. 168 p.
   Elements of library classification are examined through concrete examples and experience. The technical terminology, the various approaches to library classification, and the canons of classification are defined and discussed. For practical classification the nine steps towards classification are explicitly described with the aid of examples.

119. Saifuddin, Muhammed Abdul Haseeb. Subject headings: a list with Colon and Dewey Classification numbers. Hyderabad, Deccan, Apex Books Concern, 1962. 128 p.
   Based on the Colon Classification, fifth edition and the Dewey Decimal Classification, edition 16. A reaction to the insufficiency of the Dewey Decimal Classification for India. Explicit directions are stated for Islamic studies, biography, geographic names, language and literature, and names.

120. Parkhi, Raghunath Shatanand. Decimal classification and Colon classification in perspective. Bombay, Asia Publishing House, 1964. 545 p.
   The features and latest developments of the Decimal Classification and Colon Classification are given along with a comparative study of these schemes. Also included are the current classificatory techniques being developed in India and elsewhere, the basic principles of the discipline of classification and a list of books containing short summaries of the Colon Classification, with examples and illustrations.

121. Gour, P. N. Hindī vishaya śirshaka-sūcī. Hindi subject headings, theory and practice. Dilli, i. e. Delhi, Bharatiya Grithalaya Sangh, 1968. 406 p.
A detailed list of subject headings in Hindi, with English translation. Accommodation made for Indian topics. Introduction in Hindi.

LIBRARY EDUCATION

122. Delhi. University. Department of Library Science. Prospectus.
Lists admission requirements and procedures, details courses offered, and notes recommended reading for the department. Hawaii has 1962-1969.

123. Hintz, Carl William. Education for librarianship in India. Urbana, University of Illinois, 1964. 32 p.
Included is a history of formal education for librarianship in India from 1911, the programs of instruction obtained from nine of the 15 universities offering these programs at the graduate level. The areas discussed are curriculum, library classification and cataloging, administration and organization.

124. India (Republic). University Grants Commission. Library science in Indian universities, report of the University Grants Commission Review Committee. Delhi, Government of India Press, Manager of Publications, 1965. 86 p.
A study covering the history of library studies in India, followed by a survey of existing facilities for training and research and their syllabuses. Areas for research in library studies are outlined. The text of the questionnaire used in the survey and a summary of replies are appended.

125. Iyengar, T. K. S. Education for librarianship in India. Chicago, 1967. 42 p.
A short study, based on a questionnaire to library schools in India and the author's own experience, describing the library situation in India today, and education for librarianship.

PAKISTAN

126. Pakistan, 1947/48- . Karachi, Pakistan Publications, 1948- .
 Divided into two major parts, the first being about Pakistan as a whole, the second, with the same subject arrangement, is concerned with the provinces and States of Pakistan. Valuable for its information on education.

127. Pakistan statistical yearbook. Karachi, Government of Pakistan Press, Manager of Publications 1952- .
 From the point of view of libraries, the most important section is that on social and cultural affairs, and here there is considerable information on education in Pakistan.

PUBLISHING

128. Elahi, Fazal and Akhtar H. Siddiqui. Union catalogue of periodicals in social sciences held by the libraries in Pakistan. Karachi, Pakistan Bibliographical Working Group, 1961. 92 p. (Pakistan Bibliographical Working Group. Publication no. 5.)
 Noting some 1000 periodical titles, is an indication of the scope of the problem of periodical imports, the size of local publication, and the relative strengths of libraries in Pakistan.

129. Pakistan. National Bibliographical Unit. The Pakistan national bibliography, 1962- . Karachi, Government of Pakistan, Directorate of Archives and Libraries, National Bibliographical Unit, 1966- .
 Includes both commercial and official publications originating in East and West Pakistan. Valuable as an indication of one year's output in Pakistan. Annual volumes for 1962 and 1968 published.

31

130. National Book Centre of Pakistan. Problems of the bookworld and how they can be solved. Karachi, 1963. 120 p.
　　Summarizes recommendations from the Seminars organized by UNESCO Project on Reading Materials.

131. National Book Centre of Pakistan. Problems of book imports in Pakistan; a survey. Karachi, 1964. 90 p.
　　A study of the book import policy of the government for books and periodicals, with research conducted by the Economic Research Academy, pointing out the problem of the shortage of foreign currency.

132. National Book Centre of Pakistan. Situation of paper in Pakistan; a survey. Karachi, 1964. 73 p.
　　Study of the supply of paper as it affects book publishing in Pakistan.

133. Salahuddin Ahmad. Reading habits of women in West Pakistan; a survey. Karachi, National Book Centre of Pakistan, 1964. 55 p.
　　Discusses the methods used to make the survey and analyzes reading interests.

134. Salahuddin Ahmad. Reading habits of men in West Pakistan; a survey. Karachi, National Book Centre of Pakistan, 1964. 56 p.
　　Describes the methods used in making the survey and analyzes the data.

135. New York. State University. International Studies and World Affairs. Book production, importation and distribution in Pakistan: a study of needs, with recommendations within the context of social and economic development. Washington, Agency for International Development, 1966. 120 p.
　　A detailed study of the textbook situation in Pakistan from primary schools through university, libraries in primary, and secondary schools, colleges and universities, book publishing, including importation and paper supply, and libraries and library education. There is a separate chapter on the activities of foreign entities, such as USIS and AID.

136. Usmani, M. Adil and Ghanuil Akram Sabzwari. Pakistan book trade directory. Karachi, Library Promo-

Pakistan

tion Bureau, 1966. 204 p.
A short survey, with statistics of the book and book-related world in Pakistan, is followed by a directory divided into East and West Pakistan, then by towns. Population and literacy rates of major towns stated. Index to names of firms.

137. Ali, S. Amjad. Bookworld of Pakistan. Karachi, National Book Centre of Pakistan, 1967. 48 p.
A discussion of publishing in Pakistan, with statistical tables, and including historical background, present problems, textbooks, official publications, bookselling and literacy.

138. National Book Centre of Pakistan. English language publications from Pakistan; a guide list. Karachi, 1967. 242 p.
Lists some 2000 books published in English, a list of publishers with their addresses, and all periodicals published in Pakistan in English. Although the coverage of books is for English only, and is selective, this provides useful information on publishing in Pakistan.

139. Pakistan book news. Rawalpindi, Ferozesons, 1968?- monthly.
Information on the book world, mostly international, but with some reference to Pakistan, with select lists of new books in English, Urdu and Bengali. Some reviews.

LIBRARIES--Periodicals

140. Pakistan library review, 1958-1964, new series 1968- .
Karachi, University of Karachi, Library Science Alumni Association, 1958- quarterly.
Covers developments in the library field in Pakistan, discussing the need for libraries, government activities, problems of bibliographical services, and different types of libraries. Abstracted in Library and information science abstracts.

141. Pakistan Library Association. Journal. Lahore, 1960-51, 1968- .
Volume 2, 1968, resuming publication, concentrates on reviewing library development in Pakistan.

LIBRARIES--Books

142. Siddiqui, Akhtar H. Library resources of Pakistan. Karachi, Institute of Public and Business Administration, 1958. 26 p.
    An official survey of library resources based on the replies received from the libraries in response to the questionnaire issued by the Pakistan Bibliographical Working Group. The text covers the historical background, National Library, university and college libraries, school libraries, public libraries, special libraries, including those attached to government departments, technical and research organizations.

143. Pakistan. Bibliographical Working Group. A guide to Pakistan libraries, learned and scientific societies and education institutions. Rev. ed. Karachi, 1960. 166 p.
    The first section lists libraries and their addresses, size of collections, their nature, annual additions; the second, educational institutions; the third museums and art galleries, the fourth learned societies and institutions, and the fifth is a biographical section for 65 Pakistan librarians.

144. Moreland, Carroll Collier. The proceedings of the seminar on the purpose and function of the library in national education. Karachi, Society for the Promotion and Improvement of Libraries, 1962. 58 p.
    A collection of articles on problems facing library development in Pakistan, discussing methods of improvement of existing libraries, promotion of establishment of public libraries, promotion of cooperation among local libraries, and provision of facilities for adult education through libraries.

145. Ghazi, Muhammad Ismail. A librarian's musings. Lahore, Ilmi Kitab Khana, 1963. 60 p.
    A study of the problems of libraries and library staff in developing countries, relating to the specific problems of Pakistan. Emphasis in the first part on book losses and mutilation.

146. Pakistan Library Association. Pakistan librarianship, 1962-63. Dacca, 1964.

Proceedings of the fifth annual conference of the
Pakistan Library Association in Dacca in January
1963, discussing library development in Pakistan.
1963/64 issue for the sixth annual conference also noted.

147. Pakistan. Planning Commission. Outline of the Third
Five-Year Plan, 1965-1970. Karachi, 1964. 248 p.
Gives comparative information for education,
among other fields, for the first, second and third
five-year plans, and proposals for allocations to
education under the Third Plan.

148. Pakistan Library Association. Pakistan librarianship,
1963-64. Lahore, 1965. 284 p.
Proceedings of the Sixth Annual Conference in Lahore,
March 1965, discussing Library development in Pakistan.

149. Khurshid, Anis and Syed Irshad Ali. Librarianship in
Pakistan: fifteen years work, 1947-1962. Karachi,
Department of Library Science, University of Karachi, 1965. 65 p.
A comprehensive bibliography on librarianship and
related subjects, as publishing, in Pakistan, including books, unpublished theses, editorials and newspaper articles, published in Pakistan and elsewhere,
and mostly in English, but with materials in Urdu
and Bengali.

150. National Book Centre of Pakistan. Libraries in Pakistan: a guide. Karachi, 1968. 36 p.
Lists libraries divided into National libraries,
university libraries, college libraries, public libraries, all divided by location, and special libraries,
all divided by subject, and gives the addresses only
for special libraries.

151. Sabzwari, Ghaniul Akram. Who's who in librarianship
in Pakistan. Lahore, Library Promotion Bureau,
1969. 273 p.
In five sections, the first listing patrons of the
library movement in Pakistan, the second and main
section, librarians of Pakistan, the third, foreign
librarians in Pakistan, the fourth, who was who,
and fifth, on libraries of Pakistan. 564 individuals
listed, out of 1500 questionnaires sent out. Important librarians in former East Pakistan not noted.

152. Pakistan library directory, first edition, 1970. Dacca,

Great Eastern Books, 1970. 156 p.
751 entries for major university, academic, public and special libraries, with addresses, names of librarians, short note on the collection, usually nothing more than the number of volumes. Also included is a list of major booksellers and publishers, and a short bibliography on Pakistan librarianship.

SPECIAL LIBRARIES

153. UNESCO. South Asia Science Cooperation Office. Scientific institutions and scientists in Pakistan. New Delhi, 1958. 501 p.
The first part lists scientific organizations, the second, scientific associations, societies and technical periodicals, the third and major section is a list of scientists in Pakistan.

154. Khurshid, M. I. Need for a central (national) science library in Pakistan. Karachi, Government of Pakistan Press, 1963. 31 p.
A review of the first and second five-year plans as they relate to library development in Pakistan. These plans lay down a policy for the development of special libraries in Pakistan.

155. Mian, Tasnim Q. Principal research institutions in Pakistan. Karachi, Social Science Research Center, University of the Panjab, 1964. 2 v.
Lists 52 institutions, and excluding universities, stating the library facilities in each.

156. Symposium on Development of Scientific and Technical Libraries in Pakistan. Karachi, 1963. Development of scientific and technical libraries in Pakistan, Karachi, National Scientific and Technical Documentation Centre, 1965. 299 p.
A collection of articles reflecting the problem of scientific and technical library development in Pakistan, to emphasize the need for planned development. Despite some improvements, scientific and technical libraries are in poor condition.

157. Pakistan Association of Scientists and Scientific Professions. Scientists and technologists of Pakistan; a directory. Karachi, 1966. 367 p.

Pakistan   37

Lists over 3000 scientists and technologists, arranging these by subject field.

PUBLIC LIBRARIES

158. Seminar in the Role of the Library in the Development of the Community. Karachi, 1964. Role of the library in the development of the community. Karachi, Society for the Promotion and Improvement of Libraries, 1965. 142 p.
The seminar was held to promote the development of libraries in Pakistan, and studied administration of public libraries, their part in the development of the community, finance, legislation, and role in dissemination of knowledge.

159. Society for the Promotion and Improvement of Libraries. Karachi Public Library: a scheme. Karachi, 1967, 68 p. (SPIL Publication no. 5.)
A proposal for the establishment of a public library service in Karachi, with recommendations on standards, organization, personnel, buildings and costs.

CATALOGING

160. Khurshid, Anis. Cataloging of Pakistani names. Karachi, University of Karachi, Library Science Department, 1964. 42 p.
The study points out the linguistic confusion behind present-day Pakistani names, and makes proposals for transliteration, and gives many examples for entries.

III. SOUTHEAST ASIA

161. ASAHIL Seminar on Library Science in Southeast Asia, Bangkok 1964. Seminar on library science in Southeast Asia, Bangkok, December 18-20, 1964. Bangkok, Association of Southeast Asian Institutions of Higher Learning, 1964. 106 p.
 The Association of Southeast Asian Institutions of Higher Learning seminar papers in this publication discuss library education, location of library schools, their status and standards, library associations and placement.

162. Association of Southeast Asian Institutions of Higher Learning. Handbook of Southeast Asian Institutions of Higher Learning. Bangkok, 1967. 240 p.
 Third issue of annual edition which commenced in 1965, with up-to-date information on history, library, officers, teaching staff, curricula and facilities of member and nonmember institutions. Hong Kong is included.

163. Book publishing in Asia; report on the Regional Seminar on book publishing, held on 21-25 March 1969, in Singapore. Singapore, N.T.S. Chopra, 1970. 60 p.
 Survey of economic and technical aspects of book publishing, with special reference to the problems encountered in developing countries. Resolutions make specific proposals for Southeast Asia, the region of origin of nearly all seminar participants.

BURMA

164. Public Administration Service. Library of the Institute of Public Administration and Management, Government of the Union of Burma; annual report. Chicago, 1958-59. 2 v.
    Reports on the background of libraries in Burma, the establishment of the Institute library, and the development of its collection. Volume 2 is the final volume in the series published by the Service.

165. Gelfand, Morris A. Report of the survey of libraries of the University of Rangoon. Rangoon, 1959. 54 p.
    Object of the survey was to determine how adequately the University Libraries support the teaching and research programs of the University, with a view to making suggestions for improvement in resources and services. Conclusions and recommendations are explicitly stated.

166. Calder, Rose. A guide to library resources in Rangoon. Rangoon, Rangoon Hopkins Center for Southeast Asian Studies, Rangoon University, 1960? 47 p.
    Compiled for students and others in Burma for location of books, documents, reference works in the social sciences. Discusses library membership, library hours, library collections of the school, public, special, national and university libraries in Rangoon, and of the Government Book Depot. Includes a union list of periodicals which consists almost entirely of Western language non-Burmese serials.

167. Birkelund, Palle. Report on the development of Burmese university and research libraries. Paris, UNESCO, 1969. 21 p. (Serial no. 1186/BMS.RD/DBA.)
    Report on a visit by a UNESCO consultant 14 October to 17 December, 1968, recommending an integrated library policy under an advisory council,

and suggests its functions. The report also discusses resources, exchanges, staffing, equipment, services, and the setting up a union catalog. The annex reviews resources and staffs of individual Burmese university, college and research libraries.

INDONESIA

168. Nugroho. Indonesia: facts and figures. Djakarta, 1967. 608 p.
 Comprehensive compilation of Indonesian statistics, based on official sources, with data ranging from 1950 to 1965. Statistics are provided for public libraries, their holdings, number of newspaper titles, and circulation, periodical titles and for universities, faculties and students.

PUBLISHING--Periodicals

169. Suara penerbit Indonesia (Voice of Indonesia publishing). Djakarta, Ikatan Penerbit Indonesia, 1950?-1968 irregular.
 Information on Indonesian publishing, with slight noticing of a few current publications. Hawaii has v. 14-18.

170. Berita bibliografi (Bibliography report), 1955- . Djakarta, Gunung Agung, 1955- frequency varies.
 Lists books in Indonesian, and some Malayan books, published since 1945, and also lists bookstores and libraries with addresses.

PUBLISHING--Books

171. Ockeloen, G. Perusahaan toko buku (Manual on bookstore practice). Bandung, Gedung Buku Nasional, 1955. 128 p.
 On the theory and practice of bookselling in Indonesia, with a list of booksellers and publishers (pp. 118-128).

172. Ikatan Penerbit Indonesia (Indonesian Publishers Association). Memorandum IKAPI, lustrum ke II pada kongres kilat di Bandung, pada tgl. 23 s/d 26 No-

pember 1960 (Notes for the IKAPI Congress 23 to 26 November, 1960 at Bandung). Bandung, 1960? 160 p.
Reports on the activities of the Secretariat of IKAPI, and of its regional divisions, notes on paper distribution, and the rules of the publishers' organization.

173. Ikatan Penerbit Indonesia (Indonesian Publishers Association). Memorandum IKAPI pada Kongres ke IV di Selecta, Malang, 18 s/d 23 Maret 1963 (Notes for the 4th Congress of IKAPI, Selecta, Malang, 18 to 23 March 1963). Djakarta, 1963. 126 p.
Reports on the activities of the publishers' organization.

174. Bibliografi nasional Indonesia, kumulasi, 1945-1963. Djakarta, P. N. Balai Pustaka, 1965. 2 v.
A retrospective Indonesian national bibliography, cumulative for the years 1945-1963, with a supplement for 1964-65. Not complete, and excludes official publications, but gives an excellent overview of the publishing world from 1945 through 1965.

175. Hoetaoeroek, Maroelam. Publishing Industry in Indonesia, 1945-1965. Djakarta, IKAPI-OPS Penerbitan, 1965. 20 p.
A short discussion of the history and problems of publishing in Indonesia.

176. Ikatan Penerbit Indonesia (Indonesian Publishers Association). Kongres Kelima, tanggal 21 s/d 27 Februari 1966 di Tjipajung, memorandum IKAPI (Notes on the 5th IKAPI Congress at Tjipajung, 21 to 27 February, 1966). Djakarta, 1966. 159 p.
Reports on the activities of the publishers' organization IKAPI.

177. Ikatan Penerbit Indonesia (Indonesian Publishers Association). Kongres ke-V. IKAPI-OPS Penerbitan, 21 s/d 27 Februari 1966, di Tjipajung, (5th Congress of IKAPI at Tjipajung, 21-27 February 1966). Djakarta, Panitya Kongres ke-V, 1966. 2 v.
Papers for the Congress.

178. Ikatan Penerbit Indonesia (Indonesian Publishers Asso-

ciation). Buku kongres ke-VI IKAPI-OPS Penerbitan, Tretes, tanggal 13-17 Mei 1968 (Proceedings of the 6th IKAPI-OPS Congress, 13-17 May, 1968, at Tretes near Surabaja). Djakarta, Pengrus Umum IKAPI-OPS Penerbitan, 1968. 139, 63 p. and 2 v. supplement.
Reports for the Congress, with listings of directory type information on booksellers and publishers.

179. Wolf Management Services. Developmental book activities and needs in Indonesia. New York, USAID, 1967. 218 p.
A report of the Wolf Management Services describing the book situation at all levels of education. The problems of the paper industry, book production, marketing, book imports, are discussed. Libraries, the Library Association and library education are surveyed. Recommended solutions for problems also stated.

LIBRARIES--Periodical

180. Perpustakaan, 1954- . Djakarta, Perhimpunan Ahli Perpustakaan, Arsip dan Dokumentasi Indonesia (PAPADI) 1954- .
Bulletin published by the Indonesian Association of Librarians, Archivists and Documentalists, continuing the journal Perpustakaan volume 1 appearing in 1954. Articles are concerned with library techniques, library administration, libraries in foreign countries, and book evaluation. In Indonesian and English. No issues have appeared since 1961.

LIBRARIES--Books

181. Dunningham, A. G. W. and R. Patah. Report on a survey and recommendation for the establishment of a National Library Service in Indonesia. Djakarta, 1953. 195 p.
A dated but valuable survey of Indonesian libraries of all kinds, with recommendations for the establishment of provincial State libraries in the foundation of a national library system.

182. Tjoen, Mod Joesof. Perpustakaan di Indonesia dari

Indonesia   45

zaman ke zaman ... (The story of Indonesian libraries). Djakarta, Kantor Bibliografi Nasional, 1966. 135 p.
A short introduction to libraries under the Dutch and Japanese is followed by detailed accounts of individual libraries and bibliographical centers.

183. Indonesia. Biro Perpustakaan (Bureau of Libraries). Checklist of serials in Indonesian libraries. Djakarta, 1962. 3 v.
Lists about 6000 foreign serials in the first two volumes, and 2000 Indonesian serials in volume 3, showing holdings in 167 libraries in 19 major cities. Valuable as an indication of library strengths, and also to Indonesian periodical publishing.

184. Dunningham, A. G. W. Library development in Indonesia. n. p. UNESCO, 1964. 25 p.
Report of a UNESCO consultant in Indonesia for libraries, covering the period April 1959 to October 1963, of a project commencing in 1953. Problems of school library service, university library development, library training, and the national library system are discussed. Conclusions and recommendations given.

NATIONAL LIBRARY

185. Tairas, J. N. B. Toward a national library for Indonesia. Wellington, Library School, National Library Service, 1960. 30 p.
Discusses system of government in Indonesia and its library system, with short sections on bibliography, training of librarians and the Indonesian Library Association. Recommends that a National Library be established.

186. Museum Pusat. Perpustakaan, Djakarta (Central Museum Library). Petundjuk singkat Perpustakaan Museum Pusat (Short guide to the Central Museum Library). Djakarta, 1970. 15 p.
Discusses books, collections, library building, library hours, who may use collections, rules and regulations for the use of the collections, instruction in the use of catalogs. Floor plan of library included.

UNIVERSITY LIBRARIES

187. Williamson, William L. <u>University library development in Indonesia</u>; a report to the Ministry of Education and Culture, Republic of Indonesia. Djakarta ?, 1970. 19 p. (PIP/T 497-186-3-00218.)

    Report and recommendations discuss education of librarians, training of library assistants, provisions of materials for scholarship and teaching, encouragement of undergraduate use of libraries, and university library administration. In the last section the recommendations of previous consultants are noted, and it is suggested that directors of libraries be appointed for Indonesian universities.

SPECIAL LIBRARIES--Periodical

188. <u>Madjalah Himpunan Pustakawan Chusus Indonesia.</u> Djakarta, 1970- quarterly.

    Issued by the Association of Indonesian Special Libraries, discussing activities of special libraries in Indonesia, which are, to a great extent in the jurisdiction of the Indonesian Institute of Science.

SPECIAL LIBRARIES--Books

189. <u>Directory of scientific institutions in Indonesia.</u> Djakarta, Council for Sciences of Indonesia, 1959. 80 p. (Madjelis Ilmu Pengetahuan Indonesia. Bulletin no. 1.).

    106 scientific institutions in eight cities are listed, with addresses, objectives, publications, library collection and date of foundation stated.

190. Sutter, John Orval. <u>Scientific facilities and information services of the Republic of Indonesia.</u> Honolulu, published for the National Science Foundation by the Pacific Science Information Center, 1961, 136 p. (Pacific Scientific Information no. 1.).

    Addresses, membership and in some cases a brief history are given for ten universities, 49 institutions and 18 societies. Based on information collected in 1959.

191. <u>National Technical Documentation Center of Indonesia.</u>

Djakarta, n. d. 23 p.
Report on the objectives, function, responsibilities and activities of the PDIN (Pusat Dokumentasi Ilmiah Nasional) which was established in 1965 and located in Djakarta. Two diagrams show the structural organization of LIPI (Lembaga Ilmu Pengetahuan Indonesia) and the other of the PDIN. There is also a description of services, such as bibliography, consulting and library service offered.

192. Prawirasumantri, Kosasih. Directory of special libraries in Indonesia, 1970. Djakarta, Indonesia National Scientific Documentation Center, Indonesian Institute of Sciences, 1970. 144 p.
The fourth revised edition of a directory initially issued in 1961, listing 124 libraries, giving their Indonesian name, translated name, name of librarian, total number of volumes in the collection, subjects covered. Subject index.

193. Shank, Russell. Science and engineering library and information service development in support of research and development in Indonesia. Djakarta, 1970. 22 p.
Report of a library consultant summarizing library problems and setting goals for their solution. Recommendations for improvement of education for special librarians, their status, provision of library and information services, obtaining adequate literature resources, staffing, national library centers, translations, and network system. Also includes recommendations on publishing a union list of serials, organization of LIPI libraries and funding and building.

CATALOGING AND CLASSIFICATION

194. Tairas, J. N. B. Daftar subjek (List of subject headings). Djakarta, Jajasan Perpustakaan Indonesia, 1964. 170 p.
One of three major subject heading lists in use in Indonesia.

LIBRARY EDUCATION

195. Trimo, Soejono. <u>The education and training of Indonesian librarians.</u> Singapore, 1970. 29 p.
 Paper read at the Conference of Southeast Asia Librarians, 14-16 August, 1970, discussing the educational situation in Indonesia, the existing libraries and their personnel, and present facilities and problems in Indonesian education for librarianship.

LAOS

196. Wolf Management Services. Developmental book activities and needs in Laos. Washington, Agency for International Development, 1967. 97 p.
Surveys the background of Laos, and its natural setting, books in Lao schools, the development of the national library, and other existing libraries. Also discussed and clarified by tables of statistics is the Lao book industry, and activities of foreign agencies.

MALAYSIA AND SINGAPORE

197. Bibliografi Negara Malaysia. Malaysian national bibliography, 1967- . Kuala Lumpur, Perkhidmatan Perpustakaan Negara, Arkib Negara Malaysia, 1969- annual.
Lists titles received and registered by the National Library Service of the National Archives of Malaysia under the provisions of the Preservation of Books Act, 1966. Includes commercial and official publications, and list of names and addresses of publishers.

LIBRARIES--Periodicals

198. Perpustakaan, 1966- . Singapore, 1966- semi-annual.
Information on libraries, organization and management, in Malaysia and Singapore, activities, library training and education, news of the Persatuan Perpustakaan Malaysia and the Persatuan Perpustakaan Singapore, and on book production and distribution. Also contains information on bibliographies, book

reviews, and the annual reports of the two associations. Supersedes Perpustakaan Malaysia, 1965, which superseded in turn Malayan library journal and Madjallah perpustakaan Singapura.

LIBRARIES--Books

199. Haid, Terri J. The library situation in Malaysia. University of Pittsburgh, 1964. 83 p.
Academic exercise for a master's degree project, presumably in library science, and is divided into five sections on background, libraries, library associations, library education and financial and technical aid. Has information on school and higher education libraries, and libraries in government departments and research establishments.

200. Keeth, Kent H. A directory of libraries in Malaysia. Kuala Lumpur, University of Malaya Library, 1965. 163 p.
Lists 36 libraries in Malaysia and Singapore, and for each gives information on its administration, policy, budget, staff and salaries, buildings, book selection procedures, annual acquisition, volume of present collection, loan policy, photocopying service and address.

201. Joint Seminar of the PPM and PPS, Singapore, 1969. Planning for the '70s. Singapore, 1969. 1 v.
Papers presented on planning for development, for public, national, college and university libraries, personnel, and academic and public library buildings.

202. Lim, Edward Huck Tee. Libraries in West Malaysia and Singapore; a short history. Kuala Lumpur, University of Malaya Library, 1970. 161 p.
Surveys development of writing, printing and libraries in West Malaysia and Singapore, describing the first subscription libraries, the foreign mission libraries, university, research and school libraries. Details of history, development, book collection, periodicals, staff, budget, buildings, publications and microforms also given. Also discussed are the problems of library provision in both Malaysia and Singapore from the point of view of staff shortage and library materials processing.

Malaysia and Singapore   51

NATIONAL LIBRARY

203. Malaysia. National Archives. Penyata tahunan bagi
     Arkib Negara Malaysia (The National Archives: the
     first ten years). Kuala Lumpur, 1967. 29 p.
         The annual reports of the National Archives contain information on its history, staff, budget, acquisitions, amount of copying and reproduction done, and kind of archives deposited. The National Library Service is under the National Archives of Malaysia.

SPECIAL LIBRARIES

204. Sutter, John Orval. Scientific facilities and information services of the Federation of Malaya and the State of Singapore. Honolulu, published for the National Science Foundation, by the Pacific Science Information Center, 1961. 43 p. (P.S.I. no. 2)
         In three sections, the second listing museums, research institutions and laboratories and the facilities of the University of Malaya at Kuala Lumpur, and at Singapore.

205. Soosai, J. S. A survey of special libraries and scientific information facilities in Malaysia. n. p. 1970? 10, 3, 4, 1.
         Discusses the development of special and university libraries, indexing of Malaysian science literature, translation services, microfilming, staffing and future prospects. Appendix contains a list of West Malaysia special, university, and college libraries, noting their publications.

PUBLIC LIBRARIES

206. Anuar, Hedwig. Blueprint for public library development in Malaysia. Kuala Lumpur, Persatuan Perpustakaan Malaysia, 1968. 229 p.
         Gives details of the present public library situation with details of collections, services, staff, organization, and acquisitions, buildings, finance, and legislation. Recommends full-scale planning for the whole country, needed legislation, structure and government of public libraries, present and potential library needs.

SINGAPORE

207. Singapore (City). National Library. Singapore national bibliography, 1967- . Singapore, 1969- annual.
Lists publications received and registered in the National Library, Singapore, under the Printers' and Publishers' Ordinance of 1967 (as amended) including commercial and official publications. Maps, music, and materials in all local languages are included.

PUBLISHING

208. Singapore book world, 1970- . Singapore, National Book Development Council of Singapore, April 1970- annual, free.
Articles on publishing and allied interests and reviews of Singapore publications. Mostly in English, but with some articles and reviews in Chinese and Malay.

209. Byrd, Cecil K. Books in Singapore: a survey of publishing, printing, bookselling and library activity in the Republic of Singapore. Singapore, Chopmen Enterprises, 1970. 161 p.
Both private and public publishing is discussed, and also surveyed by language of publication. The textbook market, government participation, periodicals and market for local and foreign books, undesirable publications, pirate books and copyright, and libraries of all kinds are described.

LIBRARIES

210. Lim, Lena U Wen, Yoke-lan Wicks and Jenny Neo. Directory of libraries in Singapore. Singapore, The Library Association of Singapore, 1969. 165 p.
Contains a total of 132 libraries, including public libraries, libraries of government departments, statutory bodies, educational institutions, religious organizations, diplomatic missions and a selection of libraries in commercial firms, organizations and clubs. Information given on each library, including name of director, address, and size of collection.

Malaysia and Singapore 53

NATIONAL LIBRARY

211. Singapore (City). National Library. Report. Singapore, 1955- .
Details on services, bibliographical compilations, photo-copying, and home-reading services. Information on special service for the blind, young people, prisons, adult education, membership, issue statistics, and acquisitions also given. Supersedes in part the Report of the Raffles Museum and Library.

212. Singapore. National Library. Guide to the National Library Singapore. Singapore, 1970. 11 p.
A short pamphlet giving a chronology of the Library, list of senior staff, plans of the building, and description of services.

UNIVERSITY LIBRARIES

213. Wang, Hsiu Chin (Chen). The University of Singapore Library, its resources, services and problems. Singapore, The Library, University of Singapore, 1964. 10 p.
Describes the University of Singapore Library, with its special libraries for law, Chinese and medicine. The organization of the library is discussed, and special activities such as press cuttings and Malaysiana collection are noted.

PHILIPPINES

214. Philippines (Republic). Bureau of Census and Statistics. Yearbook of Philippine statistics, 1958- . Manila, 1958- .
Selected statistical tables on the social, political and economic conditions of the Philippines. Data based on government and private sources. The 1966 issue includes statistics on public school libraries, provincial, city and municipal libraries. Statistics on periodicals, books and pamphlets also included.

PUBLISHING

215. Philippines (Republic) Bureau of Posts. Annual report.... Manila, 1899- .
From the 1946/47 report contains a listing of Philippine periodicals and newspapers, with information on address, language, frequency and circulation. Contains some items which are not currently published.

216. Philippines (Republic). National Library. Checklist of Philippine government publications, Manila, 1958- .
A list of government publications from some 20 agencies, many of which are offered for exchange by the National Library. There is a considerable bibliography of official publications in the Philippines.

217. Wolf Management Services. Developmental book activities and needs in the Philippines. Washington. Agency for International Development, 1966. 134 p.
Evaluation of developmental book activity in the Philippines, covering books and materials relating to the educational process, books used by individuals for learning enrichment, and for technical and

218. Quezon, Philippines. University of the Philippines. Library. Filipiniana '68. Quezon City, 1969. 2 v.
Classified catalog of Filipiniana books and pamphlets in the University of the Philippines Library, noting some 9843 books and pamphlets. Periodicals and newspapers excluded. Helps to provide some estimate of the volume of Philippine book publication.

219. Quezon, Philippines. University of the Philippines. Library. Union checklist of Filipiniana serials in the libraries of the University of the Philippines, as of 1968. Quezon City, 1969. 383 p. (Research guide no. 5.)
Updates an earlier checklist published in 1962 which listed 1701 titles. 681 additional titles were added for the period 1963-1967. Also included is a list of Philippine newspapers available in the Library in 1969.

LIBRARIES--Bibliography

220. Mercado, Filomena C. Philippine libraries and librarianship, a bibliography. Manila, 1969. 57 p.
574 entries for books and periodical articles on acquisition of library materials, library services, librarianship, library associations and the development of libraries in the Philippines. The last section being further divided into sections for the National Library, public libraries, school libraries, special libraries, and university and college libraries. A draft revision of the 1964 edition, in process of further revision.

LIBRARIES--Periodicals

221. ASLP bulletin, 1954, 1956- . Manila, 1954- 1956- quarterly.
Published by the Association of Special Libraries of the Philippines, comprises articles on librarianship, library activities and book reviews. Abstracted in Library and information science abstracts.

222. Philippine Library Association. Bulletin, v. 1 (new series)- . Manila, 1965- .
 Restricted to problems of libraries and librarianship in the Philippines.

223. Journal of Philippine librarianship, 1968- . Quezon City, 1968- semi-annual.
 Published by the Institute of Library Science of the University of the Philippines. Articles on problems concerning library techniques and others reflecting interests of librarianship in the Philippines. Abstracted in Library and information science abstracts.

LIBRARIES--Books

224. Philippines (Republic) National Institute of Science and Technology. Division of Documentation. Philippine libraries. Manila, 1961-62. 2 v.
 Directory of Philippine libraries, the first volume listing 935 libraries and the second describing briefly the main and branch libraries of 25 Philippine universities.

NATIONAL LIBRARY

225. Guzman, Abraham C. de. Focus on the National Library. Manila, National Library, 1964. 136 p.
 A compilation of papers presented by division chiefs on the functions and policies of their respective divisions, such as catalog, book selection, acquisition, Filipiniana, public documents, gifts and exchanges, research and bibliography, general reference and extension.

226. Philippines (Republic). National Library. Development Plan Committee. The National Library service and development plan. Manila, 1967. 98 p.
 A survey of the Library's background, administration, resources, technical services, building, personnel, finance, extension services, with recommendations and present and future plans.

UNIVERSITY LIBRARIES

227. Swank, Raynard Coe. The libraries of the University of the Philippines; a survey report with recommendations. Quezon City, University of the Philippines, 1954. 109 p.
  A survey and analysis of problems of administration, technical services, readers' services, departmental libraries and personnel of the libraries, with specific recommendations.

SPECIAL LIBRARIES

228. Directory of special libraries resources and facilities. Manila, 1968. pp. 31-81. (ASLP Bulletin. v. 14, no. 3-4, Sep-Dec. 1968.)
  Third edition (first edition appeared in 1957) listing 163 special libraries, with addresses, name of librarian and short description of collections. Published as a separate.

SCHOOL LIBRARIES

229. Sanchez, Concordia. Philippine school libraries, their organization and management. Manila, M.C.S. Enterprises, 1971. 172 p.
  Discusses the place of the library in Philippine education, the staffing of school libraries, collection building, technical processing, services, training in the use of school libraries, planning and equipment, public relations, standards and property accountability.

LIBRARY EDUCATION

230. Mercado, Filomena C. Education for librarianship in the Philippines. Honolulu, University of Hawaii, Graduate School of Library Studies, 1971. 98 p.
  Surveys problems of librarianship in the Philippines, with chapters on education in general, library conditions and status of the library profession, library education programs and problems, and education for Philippine librarianship.

LIBRARY BUILDINGS

231. Santa Maria, Benifredo D. Program of the proposed library building. Marawi City, Mindanao State University, 1965. 160 p.

A detailed study, discussing planning in relation to the University, the library building, its public facilities, processing services, furnishings and equipment.

THAILAND

PUBLISHING

232. Wolf Management Services. <u>Developmental book activities and needs in Thailand.</u> Washington, Agency for International Development, 1967. 160 p.
    Discusses the use of books in elementary, and secondary schools, in universities, for farmers, for adult education classes, for juveniles, and for libraries and library development. Aspects of educational uses of books includes processes for their selection, approval and distribution, scope, availability and use. The conditions of all types of libraries and their development is included. The role of non-Thai agencies is described.

LIBRARIES

233. Suthilak, Ambhanwong. <u>Libraries and librarianship in Thailand.</u> Bangkok, Department of Library Science, Faculty of Arts, Chulalongkorn University, 1967. 51 p. (Library science papers no. 5.)
    A selection of articles giving information on the function of Thai libraries in the country's development, their history, their present function and work of a committee to develop a five-year plan for libraries. Information is also given on publishing history in Thailand, on education for librarianship in Thailand and on the Thai Library Association.

234. Minaikit, Nonglak. <u>An annotated bibliography of librarianship in Thailand.</u> Bangkok, Department of Library Science, Faculty of Arts, Chulalongkorn University, 1968. 47 p. (Library science papers no. 7.)
    92 books and periodical articles in English, with a subject index and in most cases full annotations. Most of the entries are to be found in the

Chulalongkorn University Central Library.

235. Maenmad, Chavalit and Sirin Chuangchot. Khūmū bannāraksasāt (Handbook of librarianship). Phranakhōn, Kasēmbannākit [1969]. 796 p.
A standard manual for those who work in every type of Thai libraries, dealing with all aspects of librarianship. Acquisition of library materials, organization of the library and library personnel, cataloging and classification, readers' services and reference service are discussed in detail. Basic reference publications in English and Thai are introduced to the reader.

NATIONAL LIBRARY

236. Thailand. Department of Fine Arts. General guide to the Vajiranan Library and the National Museum. Bangkok, 1951. 31 p.
Only the first six pages are concerned with the National Library, and concentrate on its history.

237. Thailand. National Library. The National Library of Thailand. Bangkok, [1959]. 11 p.
A brief pamphlet outlining the history, organization, statistical data and microfilming service of the National Library.

238. Gelfand, Morris A. The National Library and library development and training in Thailand. Bangkok, UNESCO, 1962. 65 p.
Information on the National Library of Thailand, on public libraries, their administration, school libraries, training for librarianship, and the library science program at Chulalongkorn University. Other topics are the Thai Library Association, and charts and tables for the required staff for the National Library.

239. Maenmad, Chavalit. Prawat Hō samut hāeng chāt (History of the National Library). Phranakhōn, Siwaphon, 1966, 91 p.
Approximately one half of this book is concerned with the background history of the National Library. The remaining half discusses the new site of the Library, preservation of collections, their proces-

Thailand   61

sing, acquisition, and development of the Library.
Plan of Library enclosed.

SPECIAL LIBRARIES

240. McMullen, Charles Haynes. The central library services project of the Institute of Public Administration, Thammasat University. Bloomington, Institute of Training for Public Service, Department of Government, Indiana University, 1961. 70 p.
Describes the libraries of government, nongovernment, and private and their holdings in the field of public administration. Gives recommendations on the number of staff required, recruitment and relation to Institute staff members, and discusses the compilation of a union catalog of library holdings in this field.

CATALOGING AND CLASSIFICATION

241. Suthilak, Ambhanwong. Khūmū kān tham batraikān samrap nangsū phāsā Thai (Cataloging manual for books in Thai). Phranakhōn, Samakhon hong samut hāeng prathet Thai (T. L. A.), [1958]. 84 p.
The classification system is based on Dewey Decimal Classification, and the descriptive cataloging on the A. L. A. Cataloging Rules, adapted to suit Thai conditions. Each rule and explanation is followed by samples of cards.

VIETNAM

242. Vietnam. Viện Quốc-gia Thống-kế (National Institute of Statistics). Annuaire statistique du Vietnam, 1949- . Saigon, 1949- .
In the field of education, the numbers of students and faculty for the different types of education are given. Information also available on the number and circulation of newspapers and other periodicals, and for production of books by subject.

PUBLISHING

243. Hanoi. Thư-viện Quốc-gia (National Library). Mục-lục xuất bản phẩm (Catalog of published works). Hanoi, 1954- .
A listing of books and periodicals received on deposit by the National Library in Hanoi. Useful indicator of the volume of publishing in the Democratic Republic of Vietnam.

244. Vietnam. Nhà văn khô và Thư-viện Quốc-gia (Directorate of National Archives and Libraries). Sách mới Nouvelles acquisitions, 1962-68. Saigon, 1962-68.
Notes some 100 books published a year in the Republic of Vietnam, and deposited in the National Library.

245. Wolf Management Services. Developmental book activities and needs in the Republic of Vietnam. Washington, Agency for International Development, 1966. 131 p.
Contains a short assessment of the probable size of the Vietnamese book market for locally published books and imports, the nature of the Vietnamese educational system, and the role of foreign agencies in book and library development.

Vietnam 63

246. Vietnam. Nhà văn khỏ và Thư-viện Quốc-gia (Directorate of National Archives and Libraries). Thư tịch quốc gia Việt-Nam National bibliography of Vietnam, 1967- . Saigon, 1967- .
Lists books and periodicals deposited at the National Library, and like Sach moi which it succeeds, excludes official publications.

LIBRARIES

247. Hội Thư-viện Việt-Nam (Vietnamese Library Association). Niên giám thư-viện Directory of Libraries. Saigon, 1970. 62 p.
Lists 62 libraries in Saigon and Cholon, giving their library name, address and information on collections. In English and Vietnamese.

NATIONAL LIBRARY

248. Vietnam. Bộ Quốc-gia Giáo-dục (Ministry of Education). Organization and administration of the Directorate of National Archives and Libraries. Saigon, 1964. 32 p.
Describes the Directorate and its functions relating to copyright and bibliography. There is a description of the National Library, the General Library and the Annex to the Directorate at Dalat. The objectives of the Directorate are stated. In English and French.

SPECIAL LIBRARIES

249. Sutter, John Orval. Scientific and information services of the Republic of Vietnam. Honolulu, published for the National Science Foundation by the Pacific Science Information Center, 1961. 236 p. (Pacific Scientific Information no. 3).
Discussion of the background of Vietnam, Vietnamese scientific manpower and training, the physical facilities, personnel and research performed by ten scientific research institutes, with a description of their libraries.

SCHOOL LIBRARIES

250. U. S. Library Development Activity, USAID, Saigon. Tập-tuyên can-bản cho thư viện trung học bản khỏi thảo. Basic high-school library collection, preliminary edition, Saigon, 1968. 150 p.

Lists 1600 books arranged by subject, including 1000 in Vietnamese, 407 in English and 193 in French.

IV. EAST ASIA

CHINA

PUBLISHING

251. Shang-hai Shih pao k'an T'u shu kuan (Shanghai Municipal Newspapers and Periodicals Library). Shang-hai Shih pao k'an kuan Chung wen ch'i k'an mu lu, 1949-1956 (Catalog of Chinese language periodicals in the Shanghai Municipal Newspapers and Periodicals Library, 1949-1956). Shang-hai, 1956. 138 p.
The most complete list for [mainland] Chinese periodicals published to 1956, noting 1393 periodicals. Frequency, place of publication, publisher and holdings for each title stated.

252. Nunn, G. Raymond. Chinese publishing statistics, 1949-1959. Ann Arbor, Association for Asian Studies, Committee on American Library Resources on the Far East, 1960. 1 v. (Preliminary data paper no. 1.)
This work is compiled from the individual entries of the Ch'üan kuo ts'ung shu mu, and the figures for 1949 through 1954 represent stocks rather than actual production for these years. Shows detailed subject development of the publishing output.

253. Nunn, G. Raymond. Chinese periodicals, international holdings, 1949-1960, indexes and supplements. Ann Arbor, Association for Asian Studies, Committee on American Library Resources on the Far East, 1961. 2 v. (Preliminary data papers 2-3.)
Lists over 1700 [mainland] Chinese periodicals, and is the most comprehensive list compiled.

254. Nunn, G. Raymond. Publishing in mainland China. Cambridge, Mass., M.I.T. Press, 1966. 83 p. (M.I.T. Report no. 4.)
Analysis of the process of generation of manuscripts, their publication, and eventual distribution throughout China and the world. There is a chapter on libraries.

China 67

LIBRARIES--Bibliography

255. Pei-ching T'u shu kuan, Peking (National Library of Peking). T'u shu kuan hsüeh lun wen so yin (Index to library science articles). Pei-ching, Shang wu yin shu kuan, 1959. 2 v.
    Divided into two parts, the first with 5359 entries, for materials published from the end of the Ch'ing dynasty to September 1949, and the second from 1949 to December 1957, with 2037 entries. Each volume is arranged in a detailed subject order, with its own author index.

256. Wang, Cheng. T'u shu kuan hsüeh lun chu tzu liao ts'ung mu, Ch'ing Kuang-hsü 15 nien-Min kuo 57 nien (A general bibliography of library science). n. p. n. d., 190 p.
    A bibliography of mostly periodical articles, arranged in detailed subject order, with some 9000 entries, covering library and library-related subjects from 1889 to 1968. The field of librarianship is not restricted to China, but includes general articles, and articles on other countries. Four-corner system author index.

LIBRARIES--Periodicals

257. T'u shu (Book readers), 1955-1960. Pei-ching, T'u shu tsa chih she, 1955-1960.
    Superseded Tu shu yüeh pao, and is a bibliographical journal for the general public, containing book reviews, review articles and publication news. A list of new publications appears in each issue.

258. T'u shu kuan kung tso (Library work), 1956- . Pei-ching, Pei-ching T'u shu kuan, 1956- monthly.
    A library journal published for libraries up to the hsien (county) level, with reports on the activities and problems of these institutions, and frequent articles on librarianship and bibliography. Annual index in the December issue of each year.

259. T'u shu kuan hsüeh t'ung hsun (Library science bulletin), 1958-1960? Pei-ching, Pei-ching T'u shu kuan, 1957-1960?
    Published as a bimonthly prior to January 1959,

the journal was issued as an internal publication in 1957. It was intended for librarians working in universities, technical institutes, and special libraries, and contained articles on both library administration and technical organization, book reviews, and reports on bibliography work in progress at various Chinese libraries.

260. T'u shu kuan (Library). Pei-ching, Pei-ching Tu shu kuan, 1961-1965?
A professional library journal, emphasizing librarianship in China, but with some notes on libraries in other countries. Circulation of 9500 issues a month. Romanization on cover: Tushuguan.

261. Lu, Chen-ching. T'u shu kuan hsüeh tz'u tien (Library Science dictionary). Pei-ching, Shang wu yin shu kuan, 1958. 898 p. (T'u shu kuan tai tz'u tien chih 1.)
A revised edition, containing some 2000 entries.

262. Ch'üan kuo Chung wen ch'i kan lien ho mu lu, 1833-1949 (National union catalog of periodicals in the Chinese language, 1833-1949). Pei-ching, Pei-ching T'u shu kuan, 1961. 1522 p.
Periodical holdings of 50 of the largest Chinese libraries are noted. Valuable for indicating the relative strengths of these libraries, and also indicating the volume of periodical publishing for the period.

263. Au, Chih-chun Tien. American impact on modern Chinese library development. Chicago, University of Chicago, 1964. 114 p.
An unpublished M. A. thesis examines the American contribution to the Chinese library movement in the form of professional training, modernization, and modifications of library techniques from the beginning of the 20th century to about 1945.

264. Huang, Nancy Lai-shen. Library development in Communist China, 1949-1962. Chicago, University of Chicago, 1964. 114 p.
An unpublished M. A. thesis including a historical background of the Chinese library movement, the philosophy underlying the Chinese Communist library movement, the characteristics and roles

China   69

of different types of libraries, the theories and practices of classification and cataloging systems, and finally library resources and readers' services.

UNIVERSITY LIBRARIES

265. Kun, Joseph C. Higher educational institutions of Communist China, 1953-1958; a cumulative list. Cambridge, Massachusetts Institute of Technology, Center for International Studies, 1961. 50 p.
227 institutions are listed by field of study, then by the six major geographical divisions of China. Libraries are a basic element in higher educational institutions, and this list is useful for the study of the background for libraries in institutions of higher education.

SPECIAL LIBRARIES

266. Wang, Chi. Mainland China organizations of higher learning in science and technology and their publications; a selected guide. Washington, U.S. Government Printing Office, 1961. 104 p.
Identifies and describes some 700 scientific organizations and their publications. 62 libraries are grouped under the following types: national, provincial, municipal, universities and colleges, and special.

267. Nielsen, Robert B. Scientific, academic and technical research organizations of mainland China; a selective listing (revised). Washington, Aerospace Technology Division, Library of Congress, 1966. 172 p.
1260 organizations, of which 220 research institutions are subordinated to and listed under the three Chinese academies, are listed. 28 libraries and one library association are included.

268. Surveys and Research Corporation, Washington. Directory of selected scientific institutions in mainland China. Stanford, published for the National Science Foundation by Hoover Institution Press, 1970. 469 p.
Contains entries for 490 scientific institutions, with detailed information of location, personnel,

structure and publications. In addition there is a list of 1127 institutions, colleges and societies. Important as a detailed survey of the organization of science in China, but no specific mention of supporting library activity.

PUBLIC LIBRARIES

269. Kung jen Ch'u pan she, Peking (Workers' Publishing Company). Ta li kai chin kung hui t'u shu kuan kung tso (With utmost effort improve service of trade union libraries). Pei-ching, 1956. 72 p.
The documents and essays of the book point out the responsibility and purpose of trade union libraries, the importance of their work and the way to revise and strengthen their work so that their educational function can be shown. Four essays on library experience show how the trade union libraries run.

270. Wang, Julia. A study of the criteria for book selection in Communist China public libraries, 1949-1964. Hong Kong, Union Research Institute, 1968, 160 p.
Discusses the historical background of Communist public libraries, their organization, criteria for book selection, and characteristics of their book collections. Excellent bibliography in Chinese and Western languages.

CATALOGING AND CLASSIFICATION

271. Wang, Yun-wu. Chung wai t'u shu t'ung i fen lei fa (System for uniform classification of Chinese and foreign books). T'ai-pei, Shang wu yin shu kuan, Min kuo 54 [1965]. 1 v. (Wan yu wen k'u hui pao.)
First published in 1928, Wang's scheme leaves the entire Dewey scheme as it is, and provides only three additional symbols to fit in the Chinese books. The symbols are +, ++, and ±. Relative subject indexes both in Chinese and English are provided. There are also chapters on author numbers, subject headings and filing.

China 71

272. Liu, Kuo-chun. Chung-kuo t'u shu fen lei fa (A system of book classification for Chinese libraries). 2d ed. Nanking, University of Nanking Library, 1936. 147 p. (Publications of the Library, no. 2.)
First published in 1929, with subjects divided into nine classes, general works, philosophy, religion, natural sciences, applied sciences, social sciences, history and geography, philology and literature, arts. Still in use in mainland China and reprinted in 1953.

273. Ch'eng, Ch'ang-yuan. Chung wen t'u shu piao t'i fa (Subject headings for Chinese books). 2d ed. Shanghai, Shang wu yin shu kuan, 1951. 426 p.
Compiled for library use and use of filing archives and newspaper clippings. Divided into three parts, the first part deals with principles of subject headings, the second part is a discussion of different headings of over 1000 entries arranged according to the four-corner numeral system.

274. Chung-kuo Jen min Ta hsüeh, Peking. T'u shu kuan (Chinese People's University Library). T'u shu fen lei fa (Book classification scheme). 3d ed. Pei-ching, Chung kuo Jen min Ta hsüeh Ch'u pan she, 1957. 736 p.
First published in 1953; fourth edition in 1962. Political ideology is used as the framework in the scheme which is divided into 17 main classes, with a numerical base. Fourth edition contains a summary of the schedules in English.

275. Wang, Hsing-wu. T'u shu fen lei fa tao lun (Introduction to book classification). T'ai-pei, Chung hua Wen hua Ch'u pan shih yen Wei yüan hui, Min kuo [1955]. 179 p. (Hsien tai kuo min chi pen chih shih tsung shu ti san chi.)
Written for the reference use of book classifiers, and topics discussed include the purpose, theory, and essentials of book classification. Both Western and Chinese major classification schemes are introduced and criticized. The practice of classification work and rules on classification are discussed.

276. Chung-kuo K'o hsüeh yuan. T'u shu kuan (Chinese Academy of Sciences. Library). Chung-kuo K'o hsüeh yüan T'u shu kuan t'u shu fen lei fa so yin

(Index to classification scheme of the Library of
the Chinese Academy of Sciences). Pei-ching,
K'o hsüeh ch'u pan she, 1959. 708 p.
   Some 30,000 entries are included in the relative
index to the classification scheme of the Library of
the Chinese Academy of Sciences, arranged alphabetically by the pinyin system. In addition an index
of about 20,000 names of animals and plants is also
provided. Indexes by stroke count attached.

277. Lai, Yung-hsiang. Chung-kuo t'u shu fen lei fa (New
classification scheme for Chinese libraries). T'aipei, n.p. Min kuo 53 [1964]. 2 v. (Hsien tai t'u
shu kuan hsüeh tsung k'an ti i erh chung.)
   The present work consists of three parts, the
schedule, the index and the explanation. The schedule is based on Lui Kuo-chun's Chung-kuo t'u shu
fen lei fa (A system of book classification for Chinese libraries) with more subdivisions added to it.
The index is arranged according to the four-corner
numeral system with Chinese radical count. Compiled for university libraries, large public libraries
and special libraries.

HONG KONG

278. Kan, Lai-bing. Libraries in Hong Kong; a directory.
Hong Kong, Hong Kong Library Association, 1963.
98 p.
   Lists 215 libraries, giving their addresses, size
of staff, size of collection, and other information.

TAIWAN

PUBLISHING

279. Chung yang T'u shu kuan, Taipei (National Central Library). Chung hua min kuo ch'u pan t'u shu mu lu
hui pien (Catalog of publications of the Republic of
China). T'ai-pei, Min kuo 53 (1964) 2 v.
   Lists 14,000 titles deposited at the National Central Library from 1949 to 1962; a valuable indicator
of development of Chinese publishing in Taiwan.

280. Kaser, David. Book pirating in Taiwan. Philadelphia,

University of Pennsylvania Press, 1969. 154 p.
History of book pirating, followed by a study of the Taiwan situation, where American books were being published at some 15 per cent of the standard U.S. price, cutting into U.S. markets in Asia, and also becoming available to American students in the United States. This was a great help to Asian libraries, but has been a cause of irritation between Taiwan and the United States.

LIBRARIES--Periodicals

281. Chung-kuo T'u shu kuan hsüeh Hui hui pao, (Bulletin of the Library Association of China). T'ai-pei, Chung-kuo T'u shu kuan hsüeh hui, 1954.
Articles on librarianship, mostly related to the situation in Taiwan, with notes on the activities of the Library Association of China. Abstracted in Library and information science abstracts.

282. T'u shu kuan hsüeh pao (Journal of library science). Tai-pei, Shih li Tung hai Ta hsüeh T'u shu kuan, 1959- .
An important source for articles on Chinese librarianship and the study of Chinese books and manuscripts.

LIBRARIES--Books

283. Tseng, David Hsien-lin. A survey of Taiwan library service. Seattle, University of Washington, 1954. 91 p.
Master's thesis in librarianship giving historical background and a survey of legislation, government libraries, public libraries, and libraries in universities and colleges, and in schools, with an analysis of service and recommendations for a national library service.

284. Chung yang T'u shu kuan, Taipei (National Central Library). Directory of the cultural organizations of the Republic of China. 2d ed. Taipei, 1963. 142 p.
Lists some 260 museums, universities, colleges, research institutions and libraries. If a library is

noted, then the size of collection is given. 3d ed. reported published in 1970.

NATIONAL LIBRARY

285. Chung yang T'u shu kuan, Taipei (National Central Library). A report of the National Central Library of the Republic of China to the Regional Seminar on the Development of National Libraries in Asia and the Pacific Area. Taipei, 1964?. 14 p.
 A short survey, discusses the organization of the National Central Library; its acquisition policies, analyzing the collections and noting bibliographical work; exchange of publications through the Library, cataloging activities, reference services, building, professional training of librarians, and special collections.

286. Chung yang T'u shu kuan, Taipei (National Central Library). The Republic of China National Library newsletter. Taipei, 1969- .
 A useful source in English on library activities in the National Central Library, and in Taiwan libraries.

287. Fun, Winnie Ta-yen. The Taiwan Provincial Taipei Library. Cleveland, School of Library Science, Western Reserve University, 1961. 28 p.
 Gives background information, including history, circulation statistics, floor plans, and lists of newspapers and periodicals held in the Library.

JAPAN

PUBLISHING--Periodicals

288. Shuppan nyūsu (The Shuppan news). Tōkyō, Shuppan Nyūsusha, 1946- three times a month. Contains articles on Japanese publishing, writers, and trade matters. Each issue lists books published in the previous ten days. Contains a useful bibliography of articles on libraries and publishing.

289. Kokuritsu Kokkai Toshokan, Tokyo (National Diet Library). Zen Nihon shuppambutsu sōmokuroku, Shōwa 23 nemban- (Japanese national bibliography, 1948-). Tōkyō, Shōwa 26- [1951-].
Since it includes official publications as well as trade publications, it is useful as an indicator of what is available from government departments. These official publications have been included from 1959. Previous to that date they were recorded in Kanchō kankōbutsu sōgō mokuroku (Catalog of official publications).

290. Shuppan nenkan, 1951 nemban- (Publication yearbook, 1951-). Tōkyō, Shuppan Nyūsusha, Shōwa 26- [1951].
Listing of publications of previous year, arranged in order of the Nihon Decimal Classification, together with information on periodicals, publishing, and related matters. Contains an excellent bibliography of materials on publishing, libraries, etc.

291. Shuppan geppō (Publishing monthly). Tōkyō, Shuppan kagaku kenkyūjo, 1959-
A detailed review of the Japanese publishing industry, emphasizing statistical sales analysis, and covering books, monthly and weekly periodicals. Compiled by the Shuppan kagaku kenkyūjo (Publica-

tion Research Institute) of the Tōkyō Shuppan Hambai Kabushiki Kaisha (Tokyo Publications Sales Company) the leading Japanese book and periodical jobber.

PUBLISHING--Books

292. Iwanami Shoten, Tokyo. Iwanami shoten gojūnen (Fifty years of Iwanami Shoten publishers). Tōkyō, 1963. 602 p.
A chronological list of publications of the Iwanami Shoten, Japan's leading modern publisher, dating from 1913 to 1963, with parallel notes on developments in the Iwanami Shoten and in the Japanese publishing world.

293. Hashimoto, Motomu. Nihon shuppan hambaishi (History of Japanese publishing). Tōkyō, Kōdansha, Shōwa 29 [1964]. 774 p.
Only one-fifth of this book is concerned with publishing after 1945, and there it discusses the role of the publishers' association, the publishers under the occupation, the new jobbers, problems faced by the industry and the export of publications.

294. Nunn, G. Raymond. Modern Japanese book publishing. Tokyo, Yushodo, 1965. 36 p.
Detailed study on the publishing industry in Japan, particularly focussed on the author-publisher relationship, the publishing process, and distribution, and the influence each has on the book market in Japan.

295. Sasaki, Shigeshi. The publishing world in Japan; chronicle of its past and present situation. Tokyo, Japan Book Publishers Assoc., 1967. 106 p.
Areas of primary import are statistical information, political and social aspects of publishing, international exchange of publication, organization structure of publishers, sales and the printing and bookbinding industry. In each of these categories there are detailed charts and graphs, but most of the information does not go beyond 1965.

296. Ishikawa, Kakuzaemon. Shuppan jiten (Publishing dictionary). Tōkyō, Shuppan nyūsusha, 1971. 660 p.

Japan

International and historical in scope, but with good coverage for modern Japanese practice in publishing and related activities, with information on organization, people, procedures and technical terms.

LIBRARIES--Periodicals

297. Toshokan zasshi (Library journal). 1907- . Tōkyō, Nihon Toshokan Kyōkai, 1907- .
Monthly publication of the Japan Library Association, with each issue discussing different aspects of libraries. International news (IFLA) and other professional news reported. Abstracted in Library and information science abstracts. Indexed in Toshokan zasshi sōsakuin (Index to the Library Journal) published in 1964, and covering volumes 1-54, published from 1907 to 1960.

298. Toshokan-kai (Library world). Tenri, Toshokan kenkyūkai, 1947- bimonthly.
A journal of librarianship, but not limited to Japanese or East Asian library topics. Abstracted in Library and information science abstracts.

299. Bibiros (Biblos). Tōkyō, Kokuritsu Kokkai Toshokan Renrakubu, 1950- monthly.
Edited by the Division of Interlibrary Services of the National Diet Library, for branches and other special libraries of the National Diet Library system, with articles on Japanese libraries, and on librarianship in other countries. Abstracted in Library and information science abstracts.

300. Kokuritsu Kokkai Toshokan, Tokyo (National Diet Library). Kokuritsu Kokkai Toshokan geppō National Diet Library monthly bulletin. Tōkyō, Shōwa 36- [1961-].
Emphasis is on articles surveying libraries and library studies in Japan, with some "house" news. Abstract in Library and information science abstracts.

301. Nihon Toshokan Kyokai (Japan Library Association). Statistics on libraries in Japan. Tokyo, 1963- .

Detailed statistics for the National Diet Library, and for individual public libraries, college and university libraries.

LIBRARIES--Books

302. Tung, Lou Watanabe. Library development and status of national bibliography in Japan. Chicago, 1953. 193 p.
M. A. thesis in library science at the University of Chicago. Over half of the book is concerned with the situation before 1945, but it is valuable as an introduction. The latter half discusses internal and external reform efforts, and also the background for the National Diet Library.

303. Japan. Nihon Gakujutsu Kaigi, Tokyo (Science Council of Japan). Nihon toshokan sōran (Survey of libraries in Japan). Tōkyō, Shizen Kagakusho Kyōkai, Shōwa 29 [1954]. 582 p.
Lists 2019 libraries (1375 general, 269 university, and 375 special) arranging these by prefectures, giving their addresses, date of establishment, size of collection, subject emphases, and name of librarian. Index to library names.

304. Japan. Mombushō. Daigaku Gakujutsukyoku (Ministry of Education. Bureau of Higher Education and Science). Gakujutsu zasshi sōgōmokuroku (Union catalogue of learned periodicals). Tōkyō, Nihon Gakujutsu Shinkōkai, Shōwa 33-34 [1958-59]. 4 v.
The four volumes are: Jimbun kagaku wabunhen, 1959 nempan (Humanistic sciences, Japanese language section, 1959); Shizen kagaku wabunhen, 1959 nempan (Natural sciences, Japanese language section, 1959); Jimbun kagaku Obun hen, 1958 (Humanistic sciences, Western language section, 1958); and Shizen kagaku Obun hen, 1958 (Natural sciences, Western language section, 1958). Later editions were published for the natural sciences. Each notes holdings of a number of major academic libraries, and is a valuable indication of relative strength, and also for periodical publication in Japan.

305. Nihon Toshokan Kyōkai (Japan Library Association).

Japan 79

Toshokan shokuin meibō (Directory of librarians).
Tōkyō, Shōwa 35 [1960]. 190 p.
Lists approximately 6000 librarians arranged by
prefecture and then by library, in August 1959.
Useful for locating individual librarians and determining
the personnel structure of Japanese libraries.

306. United States Field Seminar on Library Reference
Services for Japanese Librarians, Berkeley, etc.
1959. American libraries, report of the U.S.
Field Seminar on Library Reference Services for
Japanese Librarians. Tokyo, International House
of Japan, 1960. 147 p.
Two-thirds of the report consists of discussions
of American practice, but serves to highlight Japanese
practice. The remaining third consists of reports
on Japanese libraries, public libraries, Diet
Library reference services, Japanese university
and college libraries, education for librarianship,
and publishing and libraries in Japan.

307. Nihon Toshokan Kyōkai (Japan Library Association).
Toshokan handobukku (JLA librarian's handbook).
Tōkyō, 1960. 875 p.
Divided into six major sections, a general survey,
library administration, library materials,
processing, services, and library facilities. Indexed.

308. Japan. Laws, statutes, etc. Toshokan kankei hōki
kijunshū (Standard collection of regulations for libraries).
Tōkyō, Nihon Toshokan Kyōkai, Shōwa
37 [1962]. 121 p.
Designed as a textbook to teach general principles
of librarianship and actual procedures. Listed
are the various regulations applicable to libraries
in Japan. Regulations for the administration of libraries,
financial administration, and duties of librarians
are discussed for public libraries, National
Diet Library, and university and college libraries.

309. Uemura, Chōzaburo. Toshokangaku, shoshigakujiten
(Dictionary of librarianship and bibliographical
terms). Tōkyō, Yūrindō, Shōwa 42 [1967]. 726 p.
Entries are arranged according to the Japanese

order; for each term its equivalent is given in English, French, German and Russian. Explanations in Japanese. Indexes to the terms in Japanese, English, French, German and Russian.

310. Urata, Takeo. Toshokan hō seiritsushi shiryō (Materials on the history of the establishment of the Library Law). Tōkyō, Toshokan Kyōkai, 1968. 473 p.
Contains laws and other documents relating to Japanese libraries for the pre-war period, materials on the passing of the Public Library Law of 1950, including drafts and discussion of the library situation under the Occupation, with documents in English, including the 1948 Keeney Report.

311. Siggins, Jack A. American influence on modern Japanese library development. Chicago, 1969. 117 pages.
M. A. thesis in librarianship at the University of Chicago, describing and analyzing American influence, and covering the period up to 1966. Library education and public libraries included in the study.

312. Mamiya, Fujio. Toshokan to waga shōgai (Reminiscences of my life with libraries). Tōkyō, Fujikai, 1969-71. 2 v.
A collection of articles written by, or related to the interests of Mamiya Fujio, one of Japan's leading modern library pioneers, responsible for the introduction of decimal classification, cataloging rules, and subject headings, adapted to Japanese requirements, and advocate of romanization. Mamiya was editor of Toshokan kenkyū, an influential professional periodical in pre-World War II Japan, and owner of an office and library business in Osaka.

NATIONAL LIBRARY

313. Kokuritsu Kokkai Toshokan, Tokyo (National Diet Library). Kokuritsu kokkai toshokan nempō (Annual report of the National Diet Library). 1948- . Tōkyō, 1950- .
Issues survey the organization of library services to the Diet, the ministries and the judiciary; other libraries and the public; international library ex-

Japan

change; acquisition and processing; and administration of the National Diet Library. 1948 issue contains text in English of the National Diet Library Law.

314. Kokuritsu Kokkai Toshokan, Tokyo (National Diet Library). Facts and functions of the National Diet Library. Tokyo, 1964. 29 p.
Mimeographed paper for Regional Seminar on the Development of National Libraries in Asia and the Pacific Area, 1964, held in Manila. There is an historical introduction, followed by a discussion of acquisitions, international exchange, cataloging and classification, bibliographical activities, reference and readers' services, buildings and grounds, professional training and cooperation.

315. Kokuritsu Kokkai Toshokan, Tokyo (National Diet Library). The National Diet Library: organization, functions and activities. Tokyo, 1967. 32 p.
A brief publication showing the basic functions and operations of the Library, with pictures of the various areas to give a general conception of the structure. The specific services of the Library are discussed--organization, public and technical services, building, and cooperative activities.

316. Kokuritsu Kokkai Toshokan, Tokyo (National Diet Library). National Diet Library. Tokyo, 1968. 20 p.
In both Japanese and English, including pictures to show the basic features of the Library. The Library's main functions are to serve the Diet, serve other government agencies, gain public support and establish cooperation with libraries abroad. Statistics show activities of the library.

UNIVERSITY LIBRARIES

317. Zenkoku Kokuritsu Daigaku Toshokan chō Kaigi (All-Japan Conference of Heads of National University Libraries). Daigaku toshokan no gyōmu bunseki (Analysis of university library administration). Tōkyō, Nihon Toshokan Kyōkai, 1968. 209 p.
A detailed analysis of university library administration covering organization, personnel, public re-

318. Buckman, Thomas R., Warren Tsuneishi and Yukihisa Suzuki. University and research libraries in Japan and the United States. Chicago, American Library Association, 1972. 299 p.
 Consists of a series of short papers read at the First Japan-United States Conference on Libraries and Information Science in Higher Education held in Tokyo in 1969. Useful for updating information on Japanese university libraries, cooperation among them, university library standards, library education, availability of Japanese official publications, bibliographical control at the National Diet Library, the Japan Information Center of Science and Technology, and library associations in Japan. The Japan element is a minor part of the book, most of which is devoted to American practice, which may or may not be relevant to Japanese needs.

SPECIAL LIBRARIES

319. Japanese universities and colleges, 1965-66, with national research institutes. Tokyo, Japan Overseas Advertiser Co., 1965. 475 p.
 324 universities and colleges are listed with details showing their specialities and areas of study. Research institutes attached to universities and national research institutes are also listed. Information given on libraries.

320. Nihon Dokumentesyon Kyokai (Japan Documentation Society). Tokyo. Science information in Japan. Tokyo, 1967. 192 p.
 Surveys information activity in Japan, indicating the role of government, the various types of information organizations, including libraries, and techniques, and the training of information specialists. A revision of the 1962 edition, itself a revision of an earlier United States officially originated edition published in 1959.

321. Semmon Toshokan Kyōgikai, Tokyo (Special Libraries Association). Directory of special libraries. 2d ed. completely rev. and enl. through direct en-

quiry, during 1968. Tokyo, 1969. 379 p.
Lists 1360 government, industrial, and professional organization libraries, arranging them by kind of library. Revision of Directory of research libraries (1956).

PUBLIC LIBRARIES

322. Nihon Toshokan Kyōkai (Japan Library Association). Chūshō toshi ni okeru kōkyō toshokan no unei (Administration of public libraries in small and medium-sized towns). Tōkyō, Shōwa 38 [1963]. 217 p.
A report studying capabilities of small and medium-sized public libraries, their history, and present situation, services, school and young peoples' work, administration, and library cooperation.

323. Nihon Toshokan Kyōkai (Japan Library Association). Jidō toshokan handobukku (Children's library handbook). Tōkyō, 1963. 179 p.
Discusses services for children's libraries, materials for these libraries and their arrangement, and facilities and administration.

SCHOOL LIBRARIES

324. Japan. Mombushō (Ministry of Education). Gakkō toshokan no kanri to unyō (The administration and operation of school libraries). Tōkyō, Mombushō, 1963. 399 p.
An official manual on the purpose, administration, equipment and facilities, materials and use of school libraries.

CATALOGING AND CLASSIFICATION

325. Mori, Kiyoshi. Nihon jisshin bunrui-hō (Nippon decimal classification). Tōkyō, Nihon Toshokan Kyōkai, Shōwa 36 [1961]. 734 p.
The Nihon Decimal Classification (NDC), written in Japanese and English. Class divisions are general, history, social sciences, natural sciences, engineering technology, industry, the arts, linguistics, and literature.

326. Ono, Noriaki. Tosho bunruihō shiryō teiyō (Handbook of materials for study of book classification). 2d rev. ed. Kyōto, Mine-shobō, Shōwa 39 [1964]. 194 p.
 Consists largely of classification tables, with very little explanation. Discusses the development of classification of knowledge, the different kinds of book classification, classification codes, and book marks.

327. Kokuritsu Kokkai Toshokan, Tokyo (National Diet Library). Kokuritsu Kokkai Toshokan bunruihyō (National Diet Library classification). Tōkyō, 1963-68. 6 v.
 A new classification resembling that of the Library of Congress in form, but much smaller in physical size and subject scope intensity. The first five volumes represent subject groups; each is indexed. Volume 6 is a cumulated index. Text in English and Japanese, but there is no explanatory matter or introduction in English.

328. Nihon Toshokan Kyōkai (Japan Library Association). Nihon mokuroku kisoku, 1965 nemban (Nippon cataloging rules, 1965 edition). Tōkyō, 1965. 247 p.
 Based on the prewar Nihon mokuroku kisoku compiled by the pioneering Seinen toshokanin remmei, and revised in 1952. The publication includes sample cards. Indexed.

KOREA

PUBLISHING

329. Han'guk ch'ulp'an yŏn'gam (Books in print, Korea).
Seoul, Taehan Ch'ulp'an Munhwa Hyophoe, 1957-
annual.
A list of books in print, rather than a statement of current publication. Arranged according to the Korean Decimal Classification. The issue for 1957 is titled: Ch'ulp'an yŏn'gam (Publications yearbook). In addition to the listing of publications, it also contains a survey of publishing activities, including advertisements, selling, printing, import and export of books, libraries and paper industries. There is a directory section, and a section on law related to publishing, copyright, libraries, etc.

330. An, Ch'un-gŭn. Ch'ulp'an kaeron (Introduction to publishing). Seoul, Eulyu munhwasa, 1963. 306 p.
An introduction to publishing written in an easy style through a realistic approach. Five chapters deal with the world history of books, the theory of publishing, the forms of publication, actual publishing and sales policy. Although essentially a general study, it has some valuable references to Korea.

331. Kungnip Chungang Tosŏgwan, Seoul (National Central Library). Han'guk sŏmok (Korean national bibliography, 1945-1962). Seoul, 1964. 722 p.
21, 660 books, periodicals, dissertations, maps, music scores, and government publications are listed according to the Korean Decimal Classification. Valuable as an indicator of the development of the publishing industry in Korea.

332. Wolf Management Services. Developmental book activities and needs in the Republic of Korea. Washington, Agency for International Development, 1966.

164 p.
A survey of books, materials and periodicals for educational, technical and professional purposes in Korea. The use of books in libraries, organized reference centers and book-related activities is also discussed.

333. Taehan Ch'ulp'an Munhan Hyŏphoe (Korean Publishers' Association). Books and national development, seminar report, April 27-29, 1968. Seoul, 1968. 110 p.
Books and national development, textbooks and international cooperation are discussed in relation to publishing in Korea. Many statistical tables.

LIBRARIES--Bibliography

334. Ko, Hu-sŏk. Han'guk tosŏgwan kwan'gye munhon mongnok, 1921 yŏn-1961 yŏn (Korea library literature, 1921-1961). Seoul, Ihwa Yŏja Taehakkyo Ch'ulp'anbu, 1965. 208 p.
The bibliography is in two parts, the first covering the period to 1945, and the second from 1945. The second part contains some 3000 entries for periodical articles, and is arranged by author and by subject. Bound with Korean magazine index, 1896-1945 by Soon Ja Choi.

LIBRARIES--Periodicals

335. Tosŏgwan. Bulletin of the Central National Library of Korea. Seoul, Kungnip Chungang Tosŏgwan, 1946- .
In part a house organ of the Central National Library, one of Korea's two national libraries, and part a collection of articles on Korean libraries, with some discussion of libraries outside Korea. Contents page in English. Formerly Kungnip tosŏgwan po.

336. Tohyŏp wŏlbo (KLA bulletin), 1960- . Seoul, Han' guk Tosŏgwan Hyŏphoe, 1960- monthly.
The official journal of the Korean Library Association. Each issue contains four or five articles on foreign and Korean libraries and librarianship,

Korean Library Association activities and library extension programs.

337. Kukhoe Tosŏgwan, Seoul (National Assembly Library). Kukhoe Tosŏgwan po (National Assembly Library Review). Seoul, 1964- monthly.
Covers National Assembly Library activities, lists reference materials for Legislative work, and materials useful for library administration. Each issue contains information on libraries in Korea and outside Korea.

338. Han'guk Tosŏgwan Hyŏphoe (Korean Library Association). Han'guk tosŏgwan t'onggye (Statistics on libraries in Korea), 1965- . Seoul, 1966- annual.
Valuable for library analysis, planning and policy making. The Korean Library Association gathered annual library statistics since 1955, and from 1964 they made a more careful survey, for the enforcement of the Library Law promulgated in 1963.

LIBRARIES--Books

339. Rust, Jane E. Problems in Korean library development. Pittsburgh, University of Pittsburgh Library, 1964. 33 p.
Survey of background of Korea, general education, communication media, and book production, all related to Korean libraries and the Korean library system, with its history, present situation, extent of bibliographical control, library education, and library associations.

NATIONAL LIBRARY

340. Kungnip Chungang Tosŏgwan, Seoul (National Central Library). A general catalogue of the Central National Library, Korea, 1971 1972. Seoul, 1971? 29 p.
History, objectives, organization, activities and new building plan of the Central National Library. Parallel text in Korean and English. Organization charts and statistics of the collection given for the two periods, 1923-1945 and 1945-1970.

88   Asian Libraries and Librarianship

UNIVERSITY LIBRARIES

341. An, Yŏng-ju. Han'guk e issŏsŏ taehak tosŏgwan pongsa ŭi hyogwa e kwanhan yŏn'gu (A study of effectiveness of college and university library service in Korea). Seoul, Yŏnse Taehkkyo Tosŏgwan Hakkwa, 1965. 132 p. (Yŏnse Taehakkyo tosŏgwanhak ch'ŏngso che 16-chip.)
A study of the library in higher education in Korea, with recommendations for a better integration of libraries with the instructional program. Abstract in English.

342. Yi, Ch'un-hŭi. Han'guk ŭi taehak tosŏgwan silt'ae punsŏk (A survey on the college and university libraries in Korea). Seoul, Han'guk Tosŏgwan Hyŏphoe, 1967. 107 p.
Discusses the personnel, collection organization, service and building problems of Korean college and university libraries.

SPECIAL LIBRARIES

343. Korea Scientific and Technological Information Center, Seoul. KORSTIC yoram (KORSTIC survey). Seoul, 1971. 14 p.
An illustrated short survey of KORSTIC activities in English and Korean.

344. Korea Scientific and Technological Information Center, Seoul. Documentation activities in Korea. Seoul, 1971. 64 p.
Five main chapters; the history of publishing in Korea and its present situation; an outline of the library situation; library education; the activities of the major libraries; and a discussion of KORSTIC.

PUBLIC LIBRARIES

345. Han'guk Tosŏgwan Hyŏphoe (Korean Library Association). Konggong tosŏgwan ŭi sisŏl (Facilities of public libraries). Seoul, 1966. 216 p.
A guide for the administration of public libraries which are about to be established, with an emphasis

on practicality, and applicability for library directors and staffs to use. Includes building plans, drafts, and illustrations. The appendix has texts of library laws.

346. Maŭl Mungo Ponbu, Seoul (Microlibraries Headquarters). Maŭl mungo yoram 1967-1968 (Directory of microlibraries, 1967-1968). Seoul, 1968. 372 p.
   A brief chronology and statistical summary is followed by a listing of 9850 Korean microlibraries at the end of 1967. Libraries are arranged by province, then by district and towns. Information for each library notes numbers of members and volumes.

SCHOOL LIBRARIES

347. Kyoyuk Taehak Tosŏgwanhak Tonguhoe (Education University Library Science Study Society). Hakkyo tosŏgwan (School libraries). Seoul, Kyohak tosŏ chusik hoesa, 1964. 326 p.
   Useful as a guide to the establishment of a new school library, especially an elementary school library. The book is also planned for use in a junior teachers college as a text. There is an appendix on the use of A-V materials, and on administering a class library.

348. Han'guk Tosŏgwan Hyŏphoe (Korean Library Association). Hakkyo tosogwan ŭi sisŏl (School library facilities). Seoul, 1965. 166 p.
   A detailed and well-illustrated study on school libraries for Korea, discussing buildings, equipment and plans. Includes the texts of library laws, among them the School Library Law of 1963, and standards for school libraries.

CATALOGING AND CLASSIFICATION

349. Han'guk Tosŏgwan Hyŏphoe (Korean Library Association). Han'guk sipchin pullyupyo (Korean decimal classification). Seoul, Tan'gi 4297 [1954]. 149 p.
   Tables of the Korean Decimal Classification (KDC) and relative index. In the tables, English text accompanies the Korean. The principal modi-

fication of the Dewey Decimal Classification has
been to place language before literature.

350. Yi, Chae-ch'ŏl. Chujemyŏng p'yomok p'yo (List of
Korean subject headings). Seoul, Yŏnse Taehakkyo,
1961. 498 p. (Yŏnse Taehakkyo tosŏgwanhak ch'ong-
sŏ che 7-chip.)
A detailed listing with instructions in use. Han'-
gŭl (Korean syllabary) is used, with Chinese char-
acters in parentheses. Dewey Decimal Classification
is keyed into a large number of the entries.

351. Chŏng, P'il-mo. Tosŏ pullyupŏp kaeron (Introduction
to book classification). Seoul, Sungŭi-sa, 1964.
252 p.
Developed principally as a textbook, and surveying classification systems, followed by the practice
of classification.

352. Han'guk Tosŏgwan Hyŏphoe (Korean Library Association). Han'guk mongnok kyuch'ik (Korean cataloging rules). Seoul, 1966. 139 p.
Covers subject headings, descriptive cataloging
rules and filing, and takes note of the latest international developments in cataloging.

LIBRARY ASSOCIATIONS

353. 353. Han'guk Tosŏgwan Hyŏphoe (Korean Library As-
sociation). Korean Library Association, 1971.
Seoul, 1971. 10 p.
A brief introduction to the history, organization,
activities and publications of the Korean Library
Association.

APPENDIX

SYLLABUS FOR A COURSE ON ASIAN LIBRARIES AND LIBRARIANSHIP

The following major topic areas, approximately relating to the development of the course, will be examined in relation to each major Asian country or group of countries:

1. Introduction to the course.
2. Structure of the book collection in an Asian library.
3. Background for a traditional materials collection. East Asia.
4. Background for a traditional materials collection. Southern Asia.
5. The National Library in Asia.
6. National bibliography in Asia.
7. The University Library in Asia.
8. Special libraries and science information services in Asia.
9. Public, school and community library development in Asia.
10. Some special problems in cataloging and classification.
11. The library building in Asia.
12. Professionalism, personnel and training.

13. Library cooperation; foreign aid.

1. Introduction to the course. <u>Are there special problems in Asian library development?</u> <u>Planning in the Asian environment.</u> Japan as a special case.

   A. <u>Why a special treatment for Asia?</u> It is believed that:

      Asia has special library problems of its own not encountered or recognized in the United States.

      There is sufficient interest to make the special approach valuable.

      Comparative studies may give insights to West, and for other Asian countries.

   Are these conditions really special? Were they found in the West at an earlier stage of development?

   Is not the world becoming one, and do we need differing standards and approaches to libraries?

   Impact of non-Asian librarianship on Asian libraries.

   B. <u>Examples of some special problems</u>

      Asian language materials. Difference in language. Difficulties of book format.

      Cultural differences. Asians can no longer ignore own culture and become crypto-Westerners. Libraries represent in most cases a mix. Difficulties of the mix.

      Economic differences. In United States much of the public and private capital already created. In Asia lack of resources to handle problems-- which often defy expensive "American" solutions, such as computers, microfilm, etc. But can also jump stages of development.

      Literacy--outside Japan, lack of literate populations creates different starting point.
Schools and libraries part of education process

Appendix: Syllabus 93

in building and maintaining literacy.
Personnel.
Lack of training facilities.
Professionalism less developed. Low status and pay.

Poorly developed book trade outside China, Japan, Korea. Shortage of paper, printing machinery, typography problems, copyright laws poor. Distribution problems.

Poor development of national bibliography, outside Japan and India.

Tropical climates--over half of Asia lies in this region (vs. U.S.).
70-75% relative humidity and 50 degrees F. ideal for books and man. Sun radiation. Sea corrosion. Insects and fungi. Architectural problems.

Uses of libraries different.
Less assigned reading.
Poor reference development.
Study hall problem.

Outside aid.

C. Japan as special case

Japanese libraries far to go--although most advanced in Asia? Are they a model? Can say economic tempo of Japan not yet matched in library sector.

2. Structure of the book collection in an Asian library and its administrative implications. Problems in the acquisition of non-Asian materials.

Why acquire non-Asian materials? Typical structure of an Asian book collection.
    Typical important library is national, university, special.

Even Japan by no means self-sufficient.
Inadequacy of local sources in local languages.

Importance of the foreign periodical.
Role of non-Asian periodical.
Example of mainland China.
How to secure an adequate coverage of world literature, and control it. Speed in acquisition a problem.

Importance of non-Asian government publications. Also Asian government publications.

International book trade problems.

Acquisition of non-Asian materials. Some remedies. Direct dealing with foreign booksellers vs. dealing through own booksellers.

Exchange of publications: great potential source for Asian libraries.

Donated books. UNESCO program.

A. <u>China</u>

Purchase of materials--centralized through Guozi shudian.

Channels for the international exchange of publications.

Abstracting and control of foreign scientific literature.

Organization of translation. Volume of translation.

Acquisition channels. Hong Kong role.

Taiwan

Asia Foundation programs.

Library of the Center for Business and Public Administration, Chengchi Univ.

Appendix: Syllabus 95

    National Central Library.

B. Japan

    Selection of non-Japanese materials. Priorities of the Diet Library.

    Purchase of foreign scientific material. Liberal policy of Japanese Government.

    Acquisition by exchange.

    Exchange of non-official publications.

    Distribution of scientific materials.

    Demand for Western materials.

    Tokyo Municipal Research Library.

    Administrative Management Bureau of the Prime Minister's Office Library.

    Japanese foreign book trade.

C. Korea

    Foreign book supply.

    Import channels.

    Book donation programs.

    Graduate School of Public Administration Library.

D. India

    Most foreign materials in English.

    Import control problems.

    Indian Institute of Public Administration Library.

    Central Secretariat Library.

E. Pakistan

Most libraries new.

Demand for foreign literature. Analysis of Union list of periodicals in Pakistan libraries.

Pakistan Administrative Staff College Library.

F. Indonesia

Politics and the import of foreign materials into Indonesia.

Impact of the Revolutionary War. Limited amount of foreign exchange.

Government distinguishing between kinds of books for import.

Acquisition process. Government libraries. Non-Government libraries.

G. Philippines

Dominating role of the imported American book.

H. Thailand

List of periodicals in Thammasat University Library. Analysis.

National Institute of Development Administration Library.

Thai National Documentation Center Library.

Thammasat University Library.

I. South Vietnam

Import of books and periodicals.

National Institute of Administration Library.

Appendix: Syllabus 97

3. Background for a traditional materials collection (East Asia). Contemporary publication distribution patterns and relation to library administration.

   Importance to library administrators of history of printing and publishing--not to be antiquarians, but have practical knowledge of how to
   1. Handle rare-book collection.
   2. Realize library as final step in communication chain.

   A. China

      Introduction of Western printing.

      Organization of printing and publishing to 1949.

      Publishing under Communists. The publishing plan, rationalization of the industry, development of local publishing, volume.
      The publishing house--planning, editorial, printing, paper supply, size of edition, book prices. Local publishing. Minority publishing. Periodical publishing and distribution.
      Distribution of publishing. Hsin hua shu tien. Overstocking. Retail distribution. Direct distribution. Second-hand bookstores. Market for books and periodicals. International trade in Chinese publications.

      Taiwan

      Background.

      Book production and number of firms.

      Publishing of new books, and reprinting of classics.

      Reprinting of Western works. Copyright aspect.
        Economic aspects.

   B. Japan

      Second wave of Western style printing.

      Publishing in Japan today.

The author. Author-publisher relationship. Location of authors. Translation. Types of publishing firms. Publishing costs. Special and local publishing. Distribution through wholesalers. Distribution to retail outlets. Book market and book promotion. Distribution to readers. Libraries and bookmobiles.

C. Korea

Condition in 1945. Literacy. 1945-49 boom. 1958 trend.

Present conditions: importance of textbooks. Series boom and direct sales. High level of printing technology. Distribution of textbooks. Position of bookstores. Size of market. Relation to libraries.

4. <u>Background for a traditional materials collection (Southern Asia). Contemporary publication distribution patterns and relation to library administration.</u>

Characteristics of the traditional book in Southern Asia.

1. Palm leaf--and extension to Tibetan xylographs.
2. Black books.
3. Islamic influence--the codex.

A. India

Present situation: Four centers: Bombay, Calcutta, Madras and Delhi.

Distribution problems.

UNESCO 1959 Madras Seminar problems: Discounting, pricing, localization.

B. Pakistan

Centers: Lahore, Karachi. Localization.

Appendix: Syllabus

Language problem.

C. Indonesia

Early printing. End of Dutch printing.

Number and breakdown of publications. Number of publishers and problems.

Distribution of books. The market for books.

D. Philippines

Destruction of presses in WW II.

Numbers of books published and subject breakdown. Problems faced by publishers. Poor capitalization, and poor market.

U.S. imports.

Organization of publishing and distribution.

E. Thailand

Private book industry from 1930. Rapid growth after WW II.

Competition of popular magazines.

Educational publishing.

Thai Publishers and Booksellers Association.

Bookstores and distribution. Royalties and copyright. Market for books.

F. Vietnam

Number of publishers. Distribution.

Subject breakdown of books published.

Situation in North Vietnam.

5. The national library in Asia. Development, prospects, patterns, and administration in relation to the central government.

   A. China

   Development of libraries in the modern period. Library development under the nationalists.

   A national library service under the Communists. The establishment of major regional library centers in Shanghai, Nanking and Canton.

   The National Library of Peking.

   Taiwan

   B. Japan

   Aspects of Japanese libraries.

   Image to man in street. Pervading problems.
   Shortage of qualified staff.
   Public libraries to improve service.
   Special libraries to keep up with research.

   The Imperial Library.

   The National Diet Library. Purposes and duties.

   Administration and function of the National Diet Library.

   Organization of branches in the National Diet Library.

   Reference services in the National Diet Library.

   Development of national and international cooperation.

Appendix: Syllabus 101

C. Korea

History and general problems.

National Central Library--the "official" national library.

National Assembly Library--a second national library.

D. India

History of the library movement in India.

The National Library in Calcutta.

Regional library development in major centers.

E. Nepal

A nascent library system and National Library.

F. Pakistan

The library situation.

G. Indonesia

Library development.

The Central Museum Library. State Library systems.

H. Philippines

Development of Philippine libraries.

From Bureau of Public Libraries to National Library.

I. Criteria for a national library

>Closeness to Central Treasury; better to have a direct link to Legislature than through Ministry of Education.
>One center of activities (central location).
>Legal depository all official, nonofficial publications, including those not for sale, and nonbook materials. Two copies deposit is reasonable, makes possible lending of duplicate.
>Issues national bibliography, or is closely linked to it.
>Local collection role for all materials published in and on the country.
>Translation and information center.
>Microfilming program.
>Serves research, legislature, government; should not be a public library.
>Center for the nation's libraries, inter-library loans, union catalogs, and government library system.
>International exchange center, including exchange of official publications. Depository for UN and other international organization publications.

6. National bibliography in Asia and its core role in library development. Development of cooperative bibliography.

A. General discussion

>The importance of national bibliography to libraries and to book trade.
>
>National bibliography and the national library.
>
>Problems of copyright and deposit law.
>
>Public Law 480 and national bibliography.

B. Country discussion

>China.
>
>Taiwan.

Appendix: Syllabus   103

   Japan.

   Korea.

   India.

   Indonesia.

   North and South Vietnam.

   Malaysia and Singapore.

   C. Criteria for national bibliography

   An operation of the National Library, or closely associated with it.
   Back by a deposit law--with teeth.
   Recording total output all publications, official, non-official (for sale or otherwise) regardless of language, and nonbook materials.
   Be published at frequent intervals (at least once a month) and cumulate.
   Subject arrangement, with adequate author and title indexing.
   Full information, including price and addresses of publishers.
   Current output, but arrangements for retrospective material.
   Strong liaison with copyright office.
   Link to catalog card service.
   Acquisitions of major libraries as basis for national bibliography.

7. The university library in Asia. Development, prospects, patterns and administration. Fragmentation and cooperation.

   General discussion. Comparisons between U.S., China, Japan, and Korea.

   A. China

   University Libraries in mainland China. The People's University in Peking.

Taiwan

B. Japan

History--pre-war and post-war situation.

Place of the Library in the University.

Collections, budgets, and personnel.

Library operations; processing and service.

Library cooperation.

Attitudes to the university library in universities.

Kyoto University Library; Tokyo University Library.

C. Korea

History of libraries and higher education in Korea. Impact of Japanese period.

Comparative status of libraries in Korea and elsewhere.

Administration, collections, and personnel; budgets.

D. India

Role of the University Grants Commission.

Delhi University Library.

Problems in development.

E. Pakistan

Undergraduate colleges and their libraries.

Punjab University Library, Lahore. Other libraries.

F. Indonesia

Universities and university libraries in the colonial period.

Situation to 1962.

Situation after 1962--administration and teaching procedures.

University of Indonesia Library.

G. Philippines

Background of University Library development.

University of the Philippines Library. Ateneo de Manila University Library. Santa Tomas University Library.

H. Thailand

Chulalongkorn University Library; Thammasat University Library.

I. Malaysia and Singapore

University of Malaya Library. Nanyang University Library.

University of Singapore Library.

J. Criteria for university libraries

Sufficient reading areas, sufficient materials to support curricula, long opening hours, good research collections.
Work in close cooperation with faculty
Has a library committee, of which the university librarian is a member.
Exhibits new materials and issues accessions lists.
Adequate financial support, including access to foreign currency.
Strong professionally oriented staff, including the

university librarian.

Central control under direction of the university librarian, reporting to the president of the university directly.

Photocopy service.

Participation in inter-library loan, and union listing of materials.

8. Special libraries and science information services in Asia. Administration and cooperation with university and national libraries.

   A. The general problem--how to keep abreast of world sci-tech information and documentation.

      Language problem.

      What is being done to achieve control. Bibliographical control of imports.

      Make known own minor activity and achievements.

   B. Organization--by type

      Within higher education institutions.

      Independent organizations.

      Private commercial institutes.

      Importance of medical research.

      Poor cooperation between units.

      Organizations for sci-tech information and documentation.

      Training of personnel.

   C. Japan

      General problems--development of sci-tech documentation in Japan.

      Control of Western literature. Library cooperation.

Principal organizations--Japan Documentation Society. JICST. Science Council of Japan. NDL. Japan Special Libraries Association. Patent Office.

Education for sci-tech documentation work.

Special problems--language, romanization, coordination and cooperation.

D. Korea

General problem--uncoordinated mass of activity. Mostly at low level. Need for coordination as at other points in Korean library system.

KORSTIC. NIRI.

E. India

INSDOC established 1952. Plus special libraries attached to CSIR.
INSDOC program and sections.

Documentation Research and Training Center, Bangalore.

Problems
1. Bibliographical control and coordination.
2. Inadequate language, other than English for science programs.

F. Indonesia

LIPI--Documentation work.

Distribution of special libraries in Indonesia.

The Bogor Library.

G. Philippines

General problems of poor support, coordination, etc.

NIST Largest special library--but no book of own choice since 1961.
Documentation Division.

IRRI--an atypical example.

Philippine Atomic Energy Commission Library-- well funded, but lacks facilities and trained personnel.

Proposed National Science Development Center.

H. Thailand

TNDC--role and organization.

I. Criteria for special libraries

Support research and parent body's activities.
Has good collection of current and nonbook materials, periodicals, pamphlets, microfilms.
Offers home-made indexing in supplement to standard indexes.
Has sufficient staff, budget, accommodation.
Microfilm service.
Allows outside users to have access to library.
Translation and abstracting service. Alerting service.
Cooperates in national union listing programs.

9. Public, school and community library development in Asia and associated administrative problems.

General remarks--the least developed. Fiscal base problem. Except for Japan, sorely needed to buttress education reform.

A. China

Public library situation. Coordination with national centers.

Rural libraries. Trade union libraries.

Appendix: Syllabus 109

Public libraries in the cities.

Taiwan

Library system consisting of provincial libraries, city libraries and county libraries. Some private libraries.

Personnel and fiscal problems.

School libraries.

B. Japan

History of public library movement. Han gakkō. Kashihonya.

Poor development in Meiji period.

Seinen toshokan remmei. Osaka. Situation to 1945.

Post-war development.
Personnel.
Fiscal problems and local autonomy law.
Function of public libraries not yet recognized.
Bookmobiles.
Study hall tradition. Reference service.

Coordination with school libraries.

Osaka Public Library system.

C. Korea

Problems and use of public libraries. Fiscal. Study hall.

Private reading rooms.

Village libraries and school libraries. Microlibraries.

D. South Asia

Lack of coordination and programs.

General fiscal problem. Whatever is being done is spread thin.

Situation in India, Pakistan, Ceylon.

Attempt to secure matching grant system in India.

Delhi Public Library project of UNESCO.

UNESCO Hingurakgoda rural library project in Ceylon.

Language problems.

E. Indonesia

Many projects--mass libraries, folk libraries.

State Libraries.

School libraries--general failure of programs.

F. Philippines

Problems in the establishment of public libraries and relations with National Library.

Independent system in Manila.

School library system.

G. Thailand

System still largely on paper.
Personnel targets set too low. Poor fiscal support.
No central system in Bangkok, some municipal service.

More local initiative needed to improve system.

School libraries.

Appendix: Syllabus   111

H. Criteria for public libraries

   Free services.
   Home reading facilities.
   Recreational literature as well as informational and educational materials.
   Reference and information services.
   Has sufficient staff, budget.
   Public relations.
   Keeps local collection, and local official publications.
   Adequate relations with educational apparatus.
   Part of a larger system, providing inter-library loan.
   Library legislation providing for funding.
   Presents all sides.
   Mobile libraries providing access to library.

10. Some special problems in cataloging and classification of library collections and their administrative implications.

   A. Cataloging

      Development of central cataloging systems.
      US card systems in Asia. BNB.
      National Library of Peking--pre-war and postwar systems.
      National Diet Library.
      Thailand. Thai Library Association.
      Indian National Bibliography and its influence.

      Cuttering systems and need for Asia author tables.
      Conflicts in integration of Western and Asian materials.

      Romanization problems. China. Japan and kana.
      Korea and han'gŭl. Vietnam experience.

      Transliteration - differing practices of British Museum, INB and LC and good academic practice.

      Provincialism of American practice--evidence in code, in subject headings.

B. Classification

>Expense of purchasing set of schedules and upkeep.

>Dream of true international system--will remain just that.

>No specific solutions--just awareness of the problems.
>Usual solution--Western under DC, Asian under special;
>NDL has rejected this for its own schedules.

C. Administration

>Coordination and unified schedules--cut costs.

>Centralized cataloging.

>Relative poverty of LC schedule in Asian area--in spite of modifications.
>Especially in fields of Religion and Philosophy.
>DC also poor--authorized extensions of schedules?

D. India

>DC in India holding own, in spite of deficiencies.

>Some home-made local systems.

>Ranganathan and Colon Classification.

>Transliteration problems.

E. China

>History of development of Chinese book classification and influence of four library system in Korea and Japan.

>Modern book classifications:
>San min chu i.
>Liu Kuo-chun--major modification of Dewey.
>Wang Yun-wu--ingenious supplementation of Dewey.

Appendix: Syllabus   113

>A new system--Chinese People's University system.
>
>Romanization problems.

  F. <u>Japan</u>

>Romanization problems.
>
>Nihon Decimal Classification.
>
>Role of UDC in Japan.

  G. <u>Korea</u>

>Korean Decimal Classification.
>
>Use of han'gŭl.

11. <u>The library building in Asia.</u>

>Important to have a professional librarian in the forefront of any library building development.
>
>There are special problems.
>>The library site in relation to temperature conditions.
>>
>>The Library site and earthquakes.
>>
>>Humidity, heat, glare, aridity, sea water corrosion.
>>
>>Air conditioning--partial or total.
>>
>>Exteriors of buildings and the roof.
>>
>>Equipment and book preservation.

12. <u>Professionalism, personnel and training for libraries in Asia. Administration and need for trained personnel with adequate status.</u>

A. General problem

    Status of librarians--lower than in the US. Creates problems in effectiveness at every level.

    Needed are:
        Better training facilities and programs.
        Improved recognition and certification.
        Top-level positions to professionally trained librarians.
            (But, these must meet the challenge of the many able nonprofessional higher library administrators.)

B. China

    History of library education. Boone Library School.

    Situation in mainland China.

    Taiwan

C. Japan

    Development of library education in Japan. Before the war.

    Today: Ueno School, Keio Library School, other facilities. Inservice training.

    Library Associations. Professional literature.

D. India

    History of training of librarians.

    Present facilities for library education.

    Status of librarians and the work of the University Grants Commission.

    Library associations; professional literature.

Appendix: Syllabus 115

    E. Indonesia

        Library education; training facilities.

    F. Thailand

        Library education.
        Thai Library Association.

    G. Conclusions

        Need for development of professional associations and journals.

        Need for professional training and standards--and for training at post-master's level.

13. Library cooperation. Foreign aid in Asian library development.

    A. Library cooperation

        Major areas--whatever done on major country level or regional level.

        Much should be done at the national level, and in some countries at the provincial level.

            Coordination of library activities, avoiding of unnecessary duplications, i.e., four libraries on public administration in Lahore. Two national libraries in Korea, etc.
            Duplication of bibliographical activity.
            Union listing of resources--especially of foreign science periodicals.
            Cooperative training and standards.
            Central cataloging.

    B. Foreign assistance

        ALA.

        China Medical Board.

United Board of Christian Higher Education in Asia.

USBE.

Carnegie Corporation.

Franklin Book Programs.

Rockefeller Foundation.

Ford Foundation.

Asia Foundation.

UNESCO.

U.S. Agency for International Development.

Library of Congress.

Peace Corps.

USIS.

British Council.

AUTHOR AND TITLE INDEX

Administration and organization of college libraries in India	101
Administration and organization of school libraries in India	116
Ali, S. Amjad	137
Ali, Syed Irshad	149
All India Seminar on School Libraries	115
American impact on modern Chinese library development	263
American influence on modern Japanese library development	311
American libraries, report of the U.S. Field Seminar on Library Reference Services for Japanese Librarians	306
An, Ch'un-gŭn	330
An, Yong-ju	341
Annals of library science	68
Annotated bibliography of librarianship in Thailand	234
Annuaire statistique du Vietnam	242
Annual report of the National Diet Library	313
Annual report on the National Archives of Malaysia	203
Anuar, Hedwig	206
ASAHIL Seminar on Library Science in Southeast Asia	161
Asheim, Lester	23
ASLP Bulletin	221
Association of Special Libraries of the Philippines	221
Au, Chih-chun Tien	263
Author table for Indian names	117
Avicenne, Paul	29
Bala, Satyanarayana K.	109
Basic high school library collection, preliminary edition	250
Bengal Library Association	80-81
Bengali Academy	44, 45
Berita bibliografi	170

Bibiros	299
Bibliografi nasional Indonesia, kumulasi	174
Bibliografi negara Malaysia	197
Bibliographic services throughout the world, 1960-1964	29
Bibliography, documentation, terminology	10
Bibliography of Asian studies	3
Birkelund, Palle	167
Blueprint for public library development in Malaysia	206
Bonn, George S.	39
Book development in Asia	20
Book distribution and promotion problems in South Asia	62
Book pirating in Taiwan	280
Book production, importation and distribution in Pakistan	135
Book programs sponsored by the Asia Foundation, UNESCO and USIA in the Far East	18
Book publishing in Asia	163
Book trade manual for South Asian countries	61
Books and national development, seminar report	333
Books in Singapore	209
Booktraders	56
Bookworld of Pakistan	137
Buckman, Thomas R.	318
Bulletin of the Library Association of China	281
Byrd, Cecil K.	209
Calcutta. National Library	95, 117
Calder, Rose	166
Catalogue of books and periodicals registered in the Province of E. Pakistan	41
Cataloguing of Pakistani names	160
Central library services project of the Institute of Public Administration, Thammasat University	240
Ceylon national bibliography	51
Ceylon. Office of the Registrar of Books and Newspapers	50
Chakravarty, N. C.	78, 83
Chandler, George	32
Checklist of Philippine government publications	216
Checklist of serials in Indonesian libraries	183
Ch'eng, Ch'ang-yuan	273
Chinese periodicals, international holdings, 1949-1960	253
Chinese publishing statistics, 1949-1959	252

Author and Title Index 119

Ch'ŏng, P'il-mo	351
Ch'üan kuo Chŏng wen ch'i kan lien ho mu lu	262
Chuangchot, Sirin	235
Chujemyong p'yomok p'yo	350
Ch'ulp'an kaeron	330
Chung hua min kuo ch'u pan t'u shu mu lu hui pien	279
Chung-kuo Jen min Ta hsüeh. T'u shu kuan	274
Chung-kuo K'o hsüeh yüan T'u shu kuan t'u shu fen lei fa so yin	276
Chung-kuo t'u shu fen lei fa	272, 277
Chung-kuo T'u shu kuan hsüeh Hui pao	281
Chung wai t'u shu t'ung i fen lei fa	271
Chung wen t'u shu piao t'i fa	273
Chung yang T'u shu kuan	279, 284, 285, 286
Chūshō toshi ni okeru no unei	322
Daftar subjek	194
Daigaku toshokan no jitsumu bunseki	317
Decimal classification and Colon classification in perspective	120
Delhi Library Association	85
Delhi. Public Library	107
Delhi Public Library, an evaluation report	108
Delhi. University. Department of Library Science	122
Development of libraries	43
Development of libraries and library science in India	94
Development of libraries in New India	86
Development of scientific and technical libraries in Pakistan	156
Developmental book activities and needs in Indonesia	179
Developmental book activities and needs in Laos	196
Developmental book activities and needs in Thailand	232
Developmental book activities and needs in the Philippines	217
Developmental book activities and needs in the Republic of Korea	332
Developmental book activities and needs in the Republic of Vietnam	245
Dictionary of librarianship and bibliographical terms	309
Directory of booksellers and publishers	60
Directory of Indian libraries	74
Directory of libraries	247
Directory of libraries and who's who in library profession in India	85
Directory of libraries in Malaysia	200
Directory of libraries in Singapore	210

Directory of libraries, publishers and booksellers in the city of Bombay	88
Directory of scientific institutions in Indonesia	189
Directory of scientific research institutions in India	106
Directory of selected scientific institutions in mainland China	269
Directory of special and research libraries in India	103
Directory of special libraries	321
Directory of special libraries in Indonesia	192
Directory of special libraries, resources and facilities	228
Directory of the cultural organizations of the Republic of China	284
Documentation activities in Korea	344
Documentation and its facets	104
Dunningham, A. G. W.	181, 184

The Eastern librarian	42
The education and training of Indonesian librarians	195
Education for librarianship in India	123, 125
Education for librarianship in the Philippines	230
Elahi, Fazal	128
Elements of library classification	118
Encyclopedia of library and information sciences	27
English language publications from Pakistan	138
Exchange of ideas, East and West meet the challenge	40

Facts and functions of the National Diet Library	314
Far East and Australasia; a survey and directory of Asia and the Pacific	16
Filipiniana '68	218
Focus on the National Library	225
Franklin Book Programs	8
Free book service for all	25
Fun, Winnie Ta-yen	287

Gakkō toshokan no kanri to unyō	324
Gakujutsu zasshi sōgōmokuroku	304
Gardner, Frank M.	108
Gelfand, Morris A.	34, 165, 238
General bibliography of library science	256
General catalogue of the Central National Library, Korea	340
General guide to the Vajiranan Library and the	

Author and Title Index

National Museum	236
Ghazi, Muhammad Ismail	145
Gour, P. N.	121
Government publications of India	63
Guide to library resources in Rangoon	166
Guide to national bibliographical centres	33
Guide to Pakistan libraries	143
Guide to the National Library Singapore	210
Guide to the world's abstracting and indexing services in science and technology	36
Guzman, Abraham C. de	225
Haid, Terri J.	199
Hakkyo tosŏgwan	347
Hakkyo tosŏgwan ŭi sisŏl	348
Handbook of comparative librarianship	30
Handbook of Southeast Asia Institutions of Higher Learning	162
Handbook of universities in India	97
Han'guk ch'ulp'an yŏn'gam	329
Han'guk e issŏsŏ taehak tosŏgwan pangsa ŭi hyogwa e kwanhan yŏn'gu	341
Han'guk mongnok kyuch'ik	352
Han'guk sipchin pullyupyo	349
Han'guk sŏmok	331
Han'guk Tosŏgwan Hyŏphoe	338, 345, 348, 349, 352, 353
Han'guk tosŏgwan illam	338
Han'guk tosŏgwan kwan'gye munhon mongnok	334
Han'guk ŭi taehak tosŏgwan siltae punsok	342
Hanoi. Thư-viện Quốc-gia	243
Hashimoto, Notomu	293
Herald of library science	72
Higher educational institutions of Communist China	265
Hindi vishaya sirshaka-suci	121
Hintz, Carl William	123
Hoetaoeroek, Maroelam	175
Hội Thư-viện Việt-Nam	247
Hollister, John N.	59
Huang, Nancy Lai-shen	264
Hulbert, James A.	43
Huq, A. M. Abdul	48
Ikatan Penerbit Indonesia	172, 173, 176, 177, 178
India. Office of the Registrar of Newspapers	54

India. Planning Commission. Working Group on
   Libraries 111
India. University Grants Commission 97, 99, 124
Indian Association of Special libraries and
   Information Centres 71, 93, 102, 103
Indian books; a yearly bibliography 58
Indian Council for Library Development 89
Indian librarian 67
Indian Library Association 69, 73-75, 87
Indian library directory 75
Indian library literature 65
Indian library literature; an annotated bibliography 66
Indian national bibliography 55
Indian National Scientific Documentation Centre 106
Indian publisher and bookseller 53
India's National Library 96
Indonesia. Biro Perpustakaan 183
Indonesia; facts and figures 168
Indonesian Publishers' Association 172, 173, 176, 177, 178
International Federation for Documentation 4
International library directory 26
International library review 15
Ishikawa, Kakuzaemon 296
Iwanami Shoten gojūnen 292
Iyengar, T. K. S. 125

JLA librarian's handbook 307
Japan. Laws, statutes, etc. 308
Japan. Mombushō. 324
Japan. Mombushō. Daigaku Gakujutsukyoku 304
Japan. Nihon Gakujutsu Kaigi 303
Japanese universities and colleges, 1965-66 319
Jidō toshokan handobukku 323
Joint Seminar of the PPN and PPS 201
Journal of library science 282
Journal of Philippine librarianship 223

KORSTIC yoram 343
Kalia, D. R. 84
Kan, Lai-bing 278
Karachi Public Library: a scheme 159
Kaser, David 28, 280
Kaula, Prithvi Nath 65, 76
Keeth, Kent H. 200
Kent, Allen 27

Author and Title Index   123

Kesavan, B. S.	96
Khan, Muhammed Siddiq	46
Khandaval, Vidyut N.	88
Khosla, Raj K.	91
Khūmū bannāraksasāt	235
Khūmū kān tham batraikān samrap nangsū phāsā Thai	241
Khurshid, Anis	149, 160
Khurshid, M. I.	154
Ko, Hu-sŏk	334
Kokuritsu Kokkai Toshokan	289, 300, 313
	314, 315, 316, 327
Kokuritsu Kokkai Toshokan bunruihyō	327
Kokuritsu Kokkai Toshokan geppō	300
Kokuritsu Kokkai Toshokan nempō	313
Konggong tosŏgwan ŭi sisŏl	345
Korean cataloging rules	352
Korean decimal classification	349
Korean Library Association, 1971	353
Korea Scientific and Technological Information Center	343, 344
Kukhoe Tosŏgwan po	337
Kun, Joseph C.	265
Kung jen Ch'u pan she	269
Kungnip Chungang Tosŏgwan	331, 340
Kyoyuk Taehak Tosŏgwanhak Tonguhoe	347
Lai, Yung-hsiang	277
Lancour, Harold	27
Law of public libraries in India	109
Lee, Margaret	18
Librarianship in Pakistan	149
Librarianship in the developing countries	23
Librarian's musings	145
Libraries and librarianship in Thailand	233
Libraries in fourth five-year plan	83, 84
Libraries in Hong Kong: a directory	278
Libraries in international development	14
Libraries in Pakistan: a guide	150
Libraries in the East; an international and comparative study	32
Libraries in West Malaysia and Singapore	202
Libraries of the University of the Philippines	227
Library administration	77
Library and documentation journals	4
Library and information science abstracts	2

Library development and status of national bibliography in Japan ... 302
Library development in Communist China ... 264
Library development in eight Asian countries ... 28
Library development in Indonesia ... 184
Library education and training in developing countries ... 39
Library herald ... 70
Library legislation in India ... 92
Library literature ... 1
Library movement in India ... 76, 78
Library of the Institute of Public Administration and Management, Government of the Union of Burma, annual report ... 164
Library resources of Pakistan ... 142
Library service in India today ... 80
Library service in Indian universities ... 124
The library situation in Malaysia ... 199
Library trends ... 7
Libri; international library review and communications ... 6
Lim, Edward Huck Tee ... 202
Lim, Lena U. Wen, ... 210
List of books for libraries of high schools and intermediate colleges ... 115
Liu, Kuo-chun ... 272
Lu, Chen-ching ... 261
The Lucknow Publishing House ... 59

Mackee, M. ... 30
McMullen, Charles Haynes ... 240
Madjalah Himpunan Pustakawan chusus Indonesia ... 188
Maenmad, Chavalit ... 235, 239
Mainland China organizations of higher learning in science and technology ... 266
Malaysia. National Archives ... 203
Malaysian national bibliography ... 197
Mamiya, Fujio ... 312
Maŭl Mungo Ponbu ... 346
Maŭl mungo yoram ... 346
Meeting of Experts on Book Production and Distribution in Asia ... 19
Meeting of Experts on the National Planning of Library Services in Asia ... 24
Men of library science and libraries in India ... 91
Mercado, Filomena C. ... 220, 230

Author and Title Index 125

Mian, Tasnim Q.	155
Minaikit, Monglak	234
Mittal, S. R.	110
Modern Japanese book publishing	294
Modern public library movement and library legislation for Punjab	113
Mookerjee, Subodh Kumar	94
Moreland, Carroll Collier	144
Mori, Kiyoshi	325
Muc-luc xuât bån phâm	243
Múseùm Pusat. Perpustakaan	186

Nagar, Lal Murari	112
National Archives: the first ten years	203
National bibliography of Vietnam	246
National Book Centre of Pakistan	130, 131, 132, 138, 150
National Diet Library	316
National Diet Library: organization, functions and activities	315
National Library and library development and training in Thailand	238
National Library of Thailand	237
National Library service and development plan	226
National Technical Documentation Center of Indonesia	191
Nayudu, M. K. R.	88
Need for a central (National) science library in Pakistan	154
The need for public library development	46
Neo, Jenny	210
New classification scheme for Chinese libraries	277
New India directory of libraries and educational institutions	82
New York. State University. International Studies and World Affairs	135
Nielsen, Robert B.	267
Nien giam thu-vien	247
Nihon Dokumentesyon Kyōkai	320
Nihon jisshin bunrui-hō	325
Nihon mokuroku kisoku	328
Nihon shuppan hambaishi	293
Nihon toshokan Kyōkai	301, 305, 307, 313, 322, 323, 328
Nihon toshokan sōran	303
Nippon cataloging rules	328
Nippon decimal classification	325
Nugroho	168

Nunn, G. Raymond 252, 253, 294

Ockeloen, G. 171
Ono, Noriaki 326
Organization and administration of the Directorate
   of National Archives and Libraries 248
Organization of libraries 79
Organizing a village library 110

Pakistan 126
Pakistan Association of Scientists and Scientific
   Professions 157
Pakistan. Bibliographical Working Group 143
Pakistan book news 139
Pakistan librarianship 146, 148
Pakistan Library Association 141, 146, 148
Pakistan library directory 152
Pakistan library review 140
Pakistan. National Bibliographical Unit 129
Pakistan national bibliography 129
Pakistan. Planning Commission 147
Pakistan statistical yearbook 127
Parkash, Dewan Ram 60
Parkhi, Raghunath Shatanand 120
Patah, R. 181
Pei-ching T'u shu kuan 255
Penyata tahunan bagi Arkib Negara Malaysia 203
Perpustakaan (Djakarta) 180
Perpustakaan (Singapore) 198
Perpustakaan di Indonesia dari zaman ke zaman 182
Perusahaan toko buku 171
Petundjuk singkat Perpustakaan Museum Pusat 186
Philippine libraries 224
Philippine libraries and librarianship; a bibli-
   ography 220
Philippine Library Association 222
Philippine school libraries 229
Philippines. Bureau of Census and Statistics 214
Philippines. Bureau of Posts 215
Philippines. National Institute of Science and
   Technology. Division of Documentation 224
Philippines. National Library 216, 226
Philippines. National Library. Development
   Plan Committee 226
Planning for the '70s 201

Author and Title Index

Prasher, Ram Gopal	66
Prawat Hō samut hāeng chāt	239
Prawirasumantri, Kosasih	192
Press in India	54
Principal research institutions in Pakistan	155
Problem of book imports in Pakistan; a survey	131
Problems of the bookworld and how they can be solved	130
Problems in Korean library development	339
The proceedings of the seminar on the purpose and function of the library in national education	144
Program of the proposed library building	231
Progress of libraries in Free India	90
Public Administration Service	164
Public libraries for Asia, the Delhi seminar	38
Public libraries in East Pakistan	47
Public library movement in Baroda	112
Publishers' monthly	57
Publishers' international directory	21
Publishers' international yearbook	11
Publishing in mainland China	254
Publishing industry in Indonesia, 1945-1965	175
Publishing world in Japan	295

Quezon. University of the Philippines Library	218, 219

Ranganathan, Shiyala Ramamrita	25, 77, 79, 104, 118
Reading habits of men in West Pakistan	134
Reading habits of women in West Pakistan	133
Reminiscences of my life with libraries	312
Report of the National Central Library of the Republic of China	285
Report on a survey and recommendation for the establishment of a National Library Service in Indonesia	181
Report on the development of Burmese university and research libraries	167
Report of the survey of libraries of the University of Rangoon	165
The Republic of China National Library newsletter	286
Role of the library in the development of the community	158
Rust, Jane E.	339

Sabzwari, Ghanuil Akram	136, 151
Sách mớ'I	244
Sadhu, S. W.	92
Saha, J.	105
Saifuddin, Muhammed Abdul Haseeb	119
Salahuddin, Ahmad	133, 134
Sanchez, Concordia	229
Sankaranarayanan, N.	62
Santa Maria, Benifredo D.	231
Sasaki, Shigeshi	295
Science and engineering library and information service development	193
Science information in Japan	320
Scientific, academic and technical research organizations of mainland China	267
Scientific documentation in South and Southeast Asia	35
Scientific facilities and information services of the Federation of Malaysia and the State of Singapore	204
Scientific facilities and information services of the Republic of Indonesia	190
Scientific facilities and information services of the Republic of Vietnam	249
Scientific institutions and scientists in Pakistan	153
Scientists and technologists of Pakistan, a directory	157
Seminar in the Role of the Library in the Development of the Community	158
Seminar of University Librarians in India, Jaipur	100
Seminar on Book Publishing, Delhi	64
Seminar on library science in Southeast Asia	161, 162
Seminar on the Development of Public Libraries in Asia	38
Seminar on the International Exchange of Publications in the Indo-Pacific Area	40
Semmon Toshokan Kyōgikai	321
Sen, N. B.	86, 90
Shanghai Shih pao k'an T'u shu kuan Chung wen ch'i k'an mu lu 1949-1956	251
Shank, Russell	193
Shuppan geppō	291
Shuppan jiten	296
Shuppan nenkan	290
The Shuppan news	288
Shuppan nyūsu	288
Siddiqui, Akhtar H.	128, 142
Siggins, Jack A.	311

Author and Title Index

Simsova, S.	30
Singapore book world	208
Singapore national bibliography	207
Singapore. National Library	207, 211, 212
Singh, Mohinder	63
Situation of paper in Pakistan; a survey	132
Society for the Promotion and Improvement of Libraries	159
Soosai, J. S.	205
Special libraries and information services in India and the U.S.A.	105
Statistical abstract of Ceylon	49
Statistical abstract of the Indian Union	52
Statistical yearbook for Asia and the Far East	13
Statistics on libraries in Japan	301
A study of Bengali Muslim names	48
A study of effectiveness of college and university library service in Korea	341
A study of the criteria for book selection in Communist China public libraries	270
Suara penerbit Indonesia	169
Subject headings: a list with Colon and Dewey Classification numbers	119
Survey of public library services in India	111
Survey of special libraries and scientific information facilities in Malaysia	205
Survey of Taiwan library service	283
Survey of the University of Delhi Library	98
Survey on the college and university libraries in Korea	342
Surveys and Research Corporation	268
Suthilak, Ambhanwong	233, 241
Sutter, John Orval	190, 204, 249
Suzuki, Yukihisa	318
Swank, Raynard Coe	227
Syed, M. A.	47
Symposium on Development of Scientific and Technical Libraries in Pakistan	156
System for uniform classification of Chinese and foreign books	271
System of book classification for Chinese libraries	272
Ta li kai chin kung hui t'u shu kuan kung tso	269
Taehan Ch'ulpan Munhan Hyophoe	333
Tairas, J. N. B.	185, 194
Taiwan Provincial Taipei Library	287

Tập-tuyên căn bản cho thư viện trung học bản khỏ'i thao	250
Thailand. Department of Fine Arts	236
Thailand. National Library	237
Thatachari, C. S. S.	61
Thư tịch quốc gia Việt-Nam	246
Tjoen, Mod Joesof	182
Tohyŏp wŏlbo	336
Tosho bunruihō shiryō teiyō	326
Toshokan-kai	298
Toshokan handobukku	307
Toshokan hō seiritsushi shiryō	310
Toshokan kankei hōki kijunshu	308
Toshokan shokuin meibō	305
Toshokan to waga shōgai	312
Toshokan zasshi	297
Toshokangaku, shoshigakujiten	309
Tosŏ pullyupŏp kaeron	351
Tosŏgwan	335
Toward a national library for Indonesia	185
Trans-Pacific Conference on Scholarly Publishing	17
Trans-Pacific scholarly publishing; a symposium	17
Trehan, G. L.	101, 113, 116
Trimo, Soejono	195
Tseng, David Hsien-li	283
Tsuneishi, Warren	318
T'u shu	257
T'u shu fen lei fa	274
T'u shu fen lei fa tao lun	275
T'u shu kuan	260
T'u shu kuan hsüeh lun chu tzu liao ts'ung mu	256
T'u shu kuan hsüeh lun wen so yin	255
T'u shu kuan hsüeh pao	282
T'u shu kuan hsűeh t'ung hsun	259
T'u shu kuan hsűeh tz'u tien	261
T'u shu kuan kung tso	258
Tung, Lou Watanabe	302
Tushuguan	260
UNESCO	10, 20, 33, 37
UNESCO bulletin for libraries	5
UNESCO Regional Centre for Reading Materials in South Asia	9
UNESCO Seminar on Scientific Documentation in South and Southeast Asia	35
UNESCO. South Asia Science Cooperation Office	153

Author and Title Index 131

UNESCO statistical yearbook	12
U.S. Library of Congress, Science and Technology Division	36
U.S. Library Development Activity. USAID. Saigon	250
Uemura, Chōzaburo	309
Union catalogue of periodicals in social sciences	128
Union checklist of Filipiniana serials	219
Union list of American serials in Indian libraries	89
United Nations. Economic Commission for Asia and the Far East	13
United States Field Seminar on Library Reference Services for Japanese Librarians	306
University and college libraries	99
University and research libraries in Japan and the United States	319
University libraries for developing countries	34
University library development in Indonesia	187
The University of Singapore Library	213
Urata, Takeo	310
Usmani, M. Adil	136
Uttar Pradesh, India. Board of High School and Intermediate Education	114

Vietnam. Bộ Quốc-gia Giáo-dục		248
Vietnam. Directorate of National Archives and Libraries		244, 246
Vietnam. Institut national de la statistique		242
Vietnam. Ministry of Education		248
Vietnam. Nhà văn khô và Thư-viện Quốc-gia		244, 246
Vietnam. Viện Quốc-gia Thống-kê		242

Wang, Cheng	256
Wang, Chi	266
Wang, Hsing-wu	275
Wang, Hsiu Chin	213
Wang, Julia	270
Wang, Yun-wu	271
West Bengal library directory	81
What people read in East Pakistan	45
What women read in East Pakistan	44
White, Carl M.	98
Who's who in librarianship in Pakistan	151
Wicks, Yoke-lan	210
Williamson, William L.	187

Wolf Management Services	179, 196, 217, 232, 245
World directory of booksellers	22
World guide to libraries	31
World guide to science information and commentation services	37
Yearbook of Philippine statistics	214
Yi, Chae-ch'ŏl	350
Yi, Ch'un-hŭi	342
Zen Nihon shuppambutsu sōmokuroku	289
Zenkoku Kokuritsu Daigaku Toshokan-chō Kaigi	317

TITLES IN CHINESE, JAPANESE, KOREAN AND THAI

235 คู่มือบรรณารักษศาสตร์

239 ประวัติหอสมุดแห่งชาติ

241 คู่มือการทำบัตรรายการสำหรับหนังสือภาษาไทย

251 上海市报刊图书館中文期刊目录

255 圖書館学論文索引

256 圖書館學論著資料總目

257 讀書

258 圖書館工作

259 图書館学通訊

260 圖書館

261 圖書館学辞典

262 全国中文期刊联合目录

269 大力改進工会圖書館工作

271 中外圖書統一分類法

272 中國圖書分類法
273 中文圖書標題法
274 图书分类法
275 圖書分類法導論
276 中国科学院图书馆图书分类法索引
277 中國圖書分類法
279 中華民國出版圖書目錄彙編
281 中國圖書館學會會報
282 圖書館學報
288 出版ニュース
289 全日本出版物総目録
290 出版年鑑
291 出版月報
292 岩波書店五十年
293 日本出版販売史
296 出版事典
297 図書館雑誌

298　図書館界
299　びぶろす
300　国立国会図書館月報
303　日本圖館總覽
304　学術雑誌総合目録
305　圖書館職員名簿
307　圖書館ハンドブック
308　図書館関係法規基準集
309　図書館学・書誌学辞典
310　図書館法成立史資料
312　圕とわが生涯
313　国立国会図書館年報
317　大学図書館の業務分折
322　中小都市における公共図書館の運営
323　児童図書館ハンドブック
324　学校図書館の管理と運用
325　日本十進分類法

326 図書分類法資料提要
327 国立国会図書館分類表
328 日本目錄規則
329 韓國出版年鑑
330 出版概論
331 한국서목
334 韓國圖書館關係文獻目錄
335 도서관
336 도협월보
337 國會圖書館報
338 한국도서관통계
341 韓國에있어서大學圖書館奉仕의效果에關한研究
342 韓國의大學圖書館實態分析
345 公共圖書館의施設
346 마을문고요람
347 學校圖書館

348 學校圖書館의 施設
349 韓國十進分類表
350 주제명표목표
351 圖書分類法槪論
352 韓國目錄規則